Business English Recipes

A creative

approach

to business

English

**Judy Irigoin
and Bonnie Tsai**

Addison Wesley Longman Limited
Edinburgh Gate, Harlow,
Essex CM20 2JE, England
and Associated Companies throughout the world.

© Longman Group Limited 1995

This book is produced in association
with Pilgrims Language Courses Limited
of Canterbury, England.

First published 1995
Second impression 1996

Set in Linotron 10/12pt Cheltenham

Produced through Longman Malaysia, TCP

British Library Cataloguing-in-Publication Data
A catalogue record for this book is available from
the British Library.

ISBN 0 582 08960-3

Acknowledgements
Page 11 from *Caring and Sharing in the Foreign
Language Classroom* 1978 by Moskowitz, published
by Heinle and Heinle Publishers; page 49 we are
grateful to Faber & Faber Ltd/Grove Atlantic Inc. for
permission to reproduce an adapted extract from
'Silence' in *Plays Three* by Harold Pinter; page 123
Image Watches, Inc.

Illustrations by Kathy Baxendale
Cover illustrated by Karen Herring

A letter from the Series Editors

Dear Teacher,

This series of teachers' resource books has developed from Pilgrims' involvement in running courses for learners of English and for teachers and teacher trainers.

Our aim is to pass on ideas, techniques and practical activities which we know work in the classroom. Our authors, both Pilgrims' teachers and like-minded colleagues in other organisations, present accounts of innovative procedures which will broaden the range of options available to teachers working within communicative and humanistic approaches.

We would be very interested to receive your impressions of the series. If you notice any omissions that we ought to rectify in future editions, or if you think of any interesting variations, please let us know. We will be glad to acknowledge all contributions that we are able to use.

Seth Lindstromberg   *Mario Rinvolucri*
Series Editor   Series Consultant

Pilgrims Language Courses
Canterbury
Kent
CT1 3HG
England

Judy Irigoin

Judy Irigoin was born and educated in the United States. She went to Morocco in 1966 with the Peace Corps, where she worked on a medical technology programme. It was during this period abroad that she started teaching and became interested in the problems of learning languages.

After marrying a Frenchman and establishing permanent residence in France, she became a freelance teacher to technical and business people in French companies. She was particularly interested in the audio-visual aspects of teaching and developed exercises, activities, and teaching notes for management training films.

In 1979, with a small group of other teachers, she founded a language school in Fontainebleau, France. She is presently co-director of the Centre Actif de Langues Vivantes and Fontainebleau Langues et Communication, both established in Fontainebleau. In this capacity she works with teams of teachers, creating and assessing new activities used in various teaching situations.

Bonnie Tsai

Bonnie Tsai was born and educated in the United States. She has taught in schools in France, England, Switzerland and Greece. She was Director of Studies for a French language school for a number of years, and it was here that she became interested in developing a learner-centred approach to specialised language learning. For the last two years she has worked as a freelance trainer, specialising in training teachers to develop and use their creativity in the classroom. In addition to this, she is a trained teacher in Suggestopedia and *Psycho-dramaturgie Linguistique*, which she thinks are highly appropriate in training business people. In the summer she is a trainer at Pilgrims in Canterbury, and is co-editor with Gerry Kenny on the 'Teachers Speak Out' series in *Practical English Teaching* magazine. She lives in Toulouse with her family, which includes her husband, daughter and two cats.

Dedication

To Seth Lindstromberg, who was so helpful when we were writing this book.

Contents

Index of activities   vi

Introduction   1

Chapter 1   General techniques   4

Chapter 2   Presenting information   13

Chapter 3   Business communication
                on the phone   44

Chapter 4   Business communication
                in writing   61

Chapter 5   Using authentic business
                documents   73

Chapter 6   Gathering information
                through listening   95

Chapter 7   Business strategies   113

Bibliography   135

Index of activities

		ACTIVITY	LEVEL	LANGUAGE FOCUS
1	**GENERAL TECHNIQUES**	1.1 Learning styles 1.2 Needs analysis 1.3 Negotiation 1.4 Feedback dialogues 1.5 The list 1.6 Keeping diaries		
2	**PRESENTING INFORMATION**	2.1 The interview (group)	Intermediate +	Asking/Answering questions
		2.2 The interview (one-to-one)	Elementary +	Answering questions Giving information
		2.3 The clock	Elementary +	Organising/Presenting personal information
		2.4 Welcome to Sobovia	Intermediate	Presentation skills
		2.5 My last trip	Elementary +	Asking questions Past tense Tag questions
		2.6 The speech	Intermediate	Public speaking skills
		2.7 The executive parking lot	Intermediate +	Problem solving Presentation skills
		2.8 News playback	Intermediate	Coordination of breathing, gestures and the spoken word
		2.9 Choosing a company name	Intermediate +	Decision making Discussing
		2.10 Let me introduce	Intermediate +	Formal introductions
		2.11 Past experiences/Future plans	Intermediate +	Listening Expressing opinions Agreeing/Disagreeing
		2.12 Workspaces	Intermediate +	Describing Discussion/Problem-solving
		2.13 Remember my name	Elementary	Pronunciation practice
		2.14 The job interview	Intermediate +	Asking/Answering questions Gathering/Clarifying information
		2.15 Masks	Elementary +	Role play
		2.16 Boss or colleague	Intermediate	Listening/Speaking Asking/Answering questions
3	**BUSINESS COMMUNICATION ON THE PHONE**	3.1 Alphabet games	Beginner +	Pronunciation Spelling practice
		3.2 Circle intonation	Elementary +	Intonation practice
		3.3 Paired dialogues	Intermediate	Speaking/Listening Intonation/Stress practice
		3.4 Back-to-back telephone messages	Lower intermediate +	Speaking Receiving/Sending messages Reported speech
		3.5 Telephone awareness interview	Elementary +	Dealing with telephone anxiety
		3.6 Outgoing calls strategy	Elementary +	Making outgoing calls
		3.7 Incoming calls strategy	Elementary +	Dealing with incoming calls
		3.8 Telephone role plays	Intermediate +	Reading authentic documents Listening/Speaking Telephoning
		3.9 Telephone treasure hunt	Elementary +	Reported speech Asking questions Gathering information Telephone practice Writing

	ACTIVITY	LEVEL	LANGUAGE FOCUS
4 BUSINESS COMMUNICATION IN WRITING	4.1 Translation game	Intermediate +	Translating languages
	4.2 Definitions	Intermediate	Defining terms
	4.3 Three objects	Intermediate	Describing objects Reading/Writing Listening/Speaking
	4.4 The instruction manual	Elementary +	Following instructions Reading/Writing
	4.5 Define my terms	Elementary	Vocabulary building
	4.6 Word associations – work	Upper intermediate	Vocabulary building Writing
	4.7 E-mail easy answer	Intermediate	Writing Awareness of e-mail
	4.8 How to grow a fax	Intermediate	Reading/Deciphering Writing a fax
	4.9 Electronic tourism	Intermediate +	Reading/Writing
5 USING AUTHENTIC BUSINESS DOCUMENTS	5.1 Simple one document warm-up	Elementary +	Extracting information Asking/Answering questions
	5.2 Upper left-hand corner	Elementary +	Prepositions
	5.3 Brochures, brochures	Intermediate +	Reading Gathering information Asking/Answering questions
	5.4 First sentence	Intermediate +	Reading/Writing
	5.5 You're fired!	Intermediate +	Awareness of writing styles in business
	5.6 Crazy instructions game	Intermediate	Giving/Understanding instructions
	5.7 Organigram	Elementary +	Asking questions Describing Listening/Speaking
	5.8 Visual interrogation	Elementary +	Asking/Answering questions Describing
	5.9 Writing on the wall	Intermediate	Gathering information Speed reading for facts
	5.10 Letters to the editor	Intermediate	Reading/Speaking Giving opinions
	5.11 Gutting the newspaper	Lower intermediate +	Reading skills
	5.12 Parallel texts	Intermediate +	Asking/Answering questions Comparing/Contrasting
	5.13 The student's document	Intermediate +	Giving a talk Listening/Note-taking
	5.14 Jigsaw puzzle note-taking	Elementary +	Listening/Note-taking Organising a text
	5.15 Advertisement stereotypes	Intermediate +	Discussing Predicting Making hypotheses
	5.16 Jumbled up titles	Intermediate	Reading Predicting Summarising
	5.17 Vocabulary, vocabulary	Intermediate	Building vocabulary Explaining
6 GATHERING INFORMATION THROUGH LISTENING	6.1 Three questions	Elementary +	Asking/Answering questions Listening
	6.2 Listening for facts	Intermediate	Basic tenses Speaking/Listening Note-taking
	6.3 Yes, I agree	Intermediate	Speaking/Listening Agreeing/Disagreeing
	6.4 Listening squares	Intermediate +	Extracting information Developing listening strategies
	6.5 Listening strategies	Intermediate +	Developing listening comprehension Awareness of listening strategies

	ACTIVITY	LEVEL	LANGUAGE FOCUS
6.6	My place of work	Elementary +	Listening/Speaking Presentation skills
6.7	Jerusalem	Elementary +	Listening/Speaking Presentation skills
6.8	Listener or speaker?	Intermediate +	Fluency practice Listening skills
6.9	Into a picture	Upper intermediate +	Listening/Speaking
6.10	Follow my instructions	Intermediate	Listening/Speaking Giving/Understanding instructions
6.11	The visitor	Elementary +	Asking questions Listening
6.12	Uses of the news	Lower intermediate +	Listening skills
6.13	Listening to discourse	Elementary +	Listening skills

7 BUSINESS STRATEGIES

	ACTIVITY	LEVEL	LANGUAGE FOCUS
7.1	Guess my object	Elementary +	Asking questions Describing
7.2	It's a deal	Elementary +	First conditionals Negotiation practice
7.3	Negotiation game	Intermediate	Persuading Negotiating
7.4	Negotiation loop	Intermediate +	Persuading/Convincing Negotiating
7.5	Your advertisement	Lower intermediate +	Personal adjectives Persuading/Convincing
7.6	Image watches	Intermediate +	Problem solving
7.7	The oracle	Intermediate +	Asking questions Decision making
7.8	Three people in a tub	Intermediate +	Decision making and discussion Comparatives Superlatives
7.9	What's important?	Intermediate +	Comparatives Superlatives Decision making and discussion
7.10	So you're starting a new business	Intermediate +	Problem solving Presentation skills
7.11	American ideas	Intermediate +	Problem solving Discussing Writing
7.12	Don't break the eggs!	Elementary +	Listening/Speaking Giving/Understanding instructions Problem solving
7.13	Creative thinking	Upper intermediate	Discussing Problem solving

Introduction

GENERAL ENGLISH V. BUSINESS ENGLISH

Communication for business and technical needs tends to be more limited in scope than general English. Essentially it involves gathering, processing, and sharing information directly related to a particular field, whereas general English leans more towards socialising and entertainment. Everyday English communication is often deeply coloured by personal opinions, attitudes, beliefs, and prejudices. In business English, however, precise communication of information is vital. We have kept this clearly in mind in designing these activities. So, while you will discover many ideas here for developing fluency in communicative settings, you will find plenty which will foster objectivity, accuracy, and conciseness in expression.

The business person and learning English

Communication games and activities are now an accepted part of EFL. Experience has proved that if learning is pleasurable there is greater involvement and recall on the part of the student. However, the use of games is less common in more specialised business and professional courses. In training teachers in ESP we find that many have a preconceived image of a business person as being middle-aged, austere, and serious; someone generally dressed in grey and, if male, always wearing a tie and carrying a briefcase (see Fig. 1).

Teachers almost invariably point out that this kind of person will never want to play games or waste time on things which aren't completely serious. They say, 'That's all right for English students, but not for business people.'

But why should business people be deprived of pleasure and success in learning just because of the way they dress or because of their specialised needs? Especially when the stress and pressure of the business world is at times overwhelming. We suspect that both teachers and students of business English courses assume the content will be boring; but nothing should be farther from the truth! Just look at the emphasis placed on creative thinking, problem-solving, team-building, games, and simulations in prestigious business schools around the world. This is the kind of training business people need in order to be successful in today's business world. Our aim has been to adapt it to the needs of the language learner. We have found that our students readily see the parallels between these activities and their work and don't miss traditional vocabulary list/grammar-based business English coursebooks in the least.

Fig. 1

The business student and the English teacher

Business people typically have a great deal of knowledge in their own field. What is generally lacking is the English they need to communicate that knowledge. In fact, in talking with business people and technicians the thing which comes across loud and clear is that they don't want or need their English teacher to teach them their job. Their desire is to be able to work in a context, structured by you, which draws on their technical expertise at the same time as it affords them language input and practice where they need it. For you this means working in partnership with your students, with you being the 'English expert' and your student the 'business expert'. This partnership works especially well when you are interested enough to be able to learn from your student as well as vice versa.

One teacher recently told us she particularly enjoys her business English classes because she herself learns so much about so many different things. As a good example of how an effective teacher/student partnership works we always tell the story of one of our students, Mr. Chouchroun. Mr. Chouchroun is a very expansive, outgoing businessman who knows everything under the sun about insuring ski-lifts. Mr. Chouchroun always has a lot of questions about the English language. As soon as he hears the answer, his whole face lights up and he exclaims, 'But that's wonderful! Now I can say . . .' and he pours forth a whole string of sentences about his work, using the new structures he has just acquired; so while Mr. Chouchroun practises his English, we learn all about insuring ski-lifts!

All too often, teachers feel daunted by their students' expertise and stick to strictly linguistic teaching, shying away from anything-'businessy' they don't feel comfortable with. We think these activities will help you to integrate your students' knowledge into their coursework.

Who is this book for?

This book is for teachers of business-orientated English courses who are looking for new ideas and supplementary material for general business coursebooks, since the latter cannot cater for individual specialities in the business world. It provides communication practice easily adaptable to different professions, countries and cultures. It is for work with commercial and business school students who do not yet have work experience and also for professionally active people who have come up against their own limits in English and know exactly which specific job-related linguistic abilities they want to improve.

You will find the activities accessible even if your experience or expertise in business is limited. They are designed to cut down on the time you spend in planning and preparation.

One-to-one

In order to reach as many different teaching situations as possible, we give, whenever feasible, a group and a one-to-one version for each activity. This is to satisfy the current trend for language training based on private lessons.

The structure of the book

In this book we offer seven chapters for use with students. Each is designed to foster teamwork with you as one kind of expert and your student as another.

The format of the book

The format is very simple. It includes:
a The name of the activity
b The level of language ability at which we feel the activity works best
c Extra material needed to do the activity
d The usual time needed for the activity
e The language or skills focus
f A step-by-step procedure plan
g Our comments and/or variations
h A one-to-one version when applicable
i Acknowledgements when the activity has been adapted from one already presented elsewhere

Bonnie Tsai
Toulouse 1994

Judy Irigoin
Chailly-en-Bière 1994

CHAPTER 1

General techniques

LEARNING STYLES

Different students have different learning styles. The more you are aware of these and are able to vary and adapt your own teaching techniques the more successes you will have. To a large extent, people's learning styles have been influenced by their past learning experiences. Even if your class is having their first experience with English, they have all been learners of something before and have all had teachers. Discussing past experiences brings home the amount of influence these experiences still have on them today.

Procedure

1 Ask students to think back and bring to mind a teacher and a classmate from their past.
2 They may wish to write down any words or short sentences they associate with these two people.
3 In small groups they tell each other what they remember.
4 Bring the group back together and discuss reactions, attitudes, and patterns which are still very much alive today.

Students bring into the classroom attitudes towards learning acquired over the years. Very often these are based on failures, real or imagined difficulties with learning, and bad memories of school in general. Once these have vanished there is room for newer and more positive experiences. To achieve this you will need to sit down and think about how you really want your classroom to be.

SOME QUESTIONS FOR YOU, THE TEACHER TO THINK ABOUT

1 In what ways can the arrangement of tables, chairs, and desks be a barrier or an asset?
2 How could this arrangement hinder or aid activities requiring movement?
3 How could I use props and other realia to create a micro-culture in the classroom?
4 How would using colour, flowers, posters, and music affect my attitude towards teaching and my students' attitude towards learning?
5 Who does what in my classroom? Is it always me who sets up the role plays or could a student take over this job?
6 How do all these points affect my students' willingness to work in groups and participate in games, mimes, and role plays?

You may well find that some of the activities in this book go against your students' acquired style of learning. Their initial reaction may be one of surprise or even rejection. In the beginning stages you will want to keep such activities quite short and make sure students understand the 'why' behind them. Through feedback dialogues (1.4) you will soon see which activities fit the learning style of a particular group and which ones are better left for another group.

NEEDS ANALYSIS   1.2

Business and professional people fix goals and objectives as an everyday part of their job. Very often advancement in their careers is in direct relation to their ability to reach these goals. So the packaging of their English course needs to adapt to your students' habit of working towards goals and objectives. If clear goals are lacking, the result can be, as one frustrated student expressed it, 'a feeling that there is no direction to the course'. Frustration can also arise from the fact that business people work within a budget and a framework of time. They are often not satisfied with course descriptions which do not include definite quantification in answer to questions like:

How long will it take me to learn English?
How much can I accomplish given the time and budget I have available?
How much will it cost me?
How many hours a week will I need to spend in class?

They need, as quickly as possible, to learn enough to communicate. The course content must be expedient and give them the language they need to fit their own professional situations. The success or failure of their company to do business may well depend on it!

A needs analysis is the beginning of the business student's training. It gives us a means of giving them more quantitative answers to the questions above. And here are a couple of advantages for the students:

- It gives them the opportunity to make choices and establish priorities for their course.
- It asks them to consider what can be accomplished in a short period and what should, instead, be long term goals. For example, the student may eventually need English to participate in discussions and meetings but today's immediate need may be to send a clear and concise fax.

Recently, we worked with a student called Peter who said he wanted to learn lots of new vocabulary. However, his immediate goals needed to be clearer for him if he was to feel he was making any progress. A task-orientated needs analysis chart like the one on page 7 (Fig. 2) helped Peter to break down his vague overall goal (knowing lots of vocabulary) into tangible professional situations in which he felt he was unable to communicate effectively.

Procedure

To use the needs analysis chart we asked Peter to:
1 Read through the chart.
2 Underline with one colour ink all the tasks he felt he could now do successfully.
3 With a different colour ink, he underlined the tasks he wanted to be able to do at the end of his course.

The tasks which fell in between made up the basis for a realistic set of goals taking into consideration Peter's level in English, the time, and the money he had to spend.

1.3   NEGOTIATION

Negotiation, like fixing goals and objectives, is another important part of what goes on in the business world. Using a needs analysis prepares you, the teacher, to take the next step. Namely, negotiating course content which is in line with your students' desires and capabilities. Too often, when forming classes and shaping courses the only criterion teachers and schools have to go by is students' ability in the language. But with only this as a guide, it is very difficult to provide a course which gives each student what they need and which motivates them to learn. By starting out with a negotiation between yourself and the group about how their time can be most effectively used, you avoid conflicts later on. Don't assume anything. In particular, face up to the reality of differences within the group from the beginning. During the first class meeting you can do an activity like NEGOTIATION.

Procedure

1 Ask everyone to write down three things they would like to be able to do by the end of their course. Encourage students to be precise and avoid goals which are too broad and vague.
2 Students mingle and compare lists to see where there are common areas in which they can work. (One in-company group found they all needed to be able to read instruction manuals more quickly, write faxes, and deal with customer questions and problems by phone.)

This provides a basis to negotiate: e.g. (a) the amount of time out of the total number of class hours they'd like to devote to each skill, (b) how individual needs within the group can be provided for, and (c) material and documents the group would enjoy working with.

NEEDS ANALYSIS CHART

Fig. 2

LISTENING AND UNDERSTANDING	QUESTIONING AND INFORMING	PRESENTING AND REPORTING	WRITING	DEVELOPMENT IN THE OUTSIDE WORLD	PLANNING, DECIDING AND DIRECTING
Can understand the theatre, films and t.v.	Have no difficulty in obtaining information from any source.	Can make presentations at high level meetings.	Can write and dictate business letters without mistakes.	Can be the host at parties and cocktails.	Can direct a meeting with complete ease.
Can understand everything except nuances and plays on words.	Can question a speaker at length.	Can deliver a short appropriate speech depending on the situation.	Can write summaries of reports.	Can tell stories and jokes with ease.	Can argue my point of view persuasively.
Can understand two people speaking their language together.	Can obtain detailed information about work and general themes.	Have a clear and precise expression.	Can write professional reports.	Can hold my own as a dinner guest.	Can present my opinions with ease.
Can understand the basic points of meetings and everyday conversations.	Can ask questions about general opinions.	Have a good facility of elocution but make mistakes.	Can write spontaneously but with a few errors.	Feel at ease at a cocktail party.	Can give suggestions and detailed proposals.
Can understand an everyday vocabulary.	Can ask questions with ease.	Can present a project in public.	Can write short reports if careful and attentive.	Can maintain a conversation at a cocktail party.	Try to find the most precise words.
Can understand the sense of sentences but lack a nuanced vocabulary.	Can obtain information but lack ease.	Can present the guidelines of a project.	Can write memos and longer business letters.	Can participate in informal meetings.	Can discuss different alternatives easily.
Can globally understand most information.	Can ask elementary questions by telephone.	Can comment on pictures.	Can write short business letters.	Try to maintain a polite conversation.	Can present and impose conditions.
Can understand a narrative of events in the past.	Can ask simple questions in the past.	Can tell a story in the past.	Can write correctly at an elementary level.	Can respond to polite requests.	Can participate in simple discussions but lack vocabulary.
Can understand simple sentences.	Can ask questions about daily activities.	Can describe daily activities.	Can fill in a simple form.	Can offer cigarettes and drinks.	Can make simple suggestions.
Can understand elementary sentences.	Can find out about prices, situations and amounts.	Can describe the position of objects and their location.	Know the alphabet and basic spelling.	Can give names, nationalities and elementary greetings.	Can give very elementary information.

By involving the class in the selection of material and documents, you are sending out clear signals that this is *their* class. In addition, you can make use of the fact that business people are always ready and willing to bring information about their company into class. From the point of view of efficiency, this means they are not wasting time on material which does not strictly conform to their interests and needs. In the long run this makes your job easier and your students happier because they feel you have tailor-made the course for them. Here is an example of the results of course content negotiated with a group (Fig. 3). As you can see, students' goals have been restructured into 'tasks' and 'components'.

TASKS	COMPONENTS	NUMBER OF CLASS HOURS
memoranda internal correspondence meetings (participant) meetings (chairman)	INTERNAL MEETINGS	8
letters faxes external correspondence	EXTERNAL CORRESPONDENCE	5
journals	RAPID READING	2
reports papers	INFORMATION PRESENTATION	3
conference participation conference–papers	CONFERENCE SKILLS	10
interviews	INTERVIEWS	2
Total		30

Fig. 3

STUDENT AUTONOMY

Another subject for negotiation is student autonomy and involvement in the class. The more students involve themselves and take responsibility, the better they learn and remember. This is true of groups and especially so with one-to-one teaching where, if you aren't careful, you can find yourself asking all the questions, creating all the activities and in general doing all the work while the student takes on a rather passive role. Explain to your students that autonomy is no longer considered the final stage in learning, but a vital part at all stages.

Negotiating student autonomy and responsibility can reach beyond the classroom. For example, students may agree to read documents or listen to cassettes at home to gain more time in class for more active communication activities.

Negotiating Classroom Conflicts

Negotiation is also a way to deal with spoken or unspoken complaints like 'We don't do enough grammar' or 'I don't like listening to cassettes'. By listening to students' opinions and feelings and being willing to use negotiation as a tool to find a compromise, you reassure them and they become more willing to accept aspects of the course which they find less enjoyable.

CLASS CONTRACTS

As an outcome of all these different negotiations, students can write up on paper a contract setting down the terms agreed upon. Like all contracts, it can come up for review from time to time.

1.4   FEEDBACK DIALOGUES

This is the name we give to the exchanges and conversations which develop between students and teachers about their English classes. It is not something which just happens, but is an integral, planned part of each course.

Guidelines to follow in setting up a feedback dialogue

1 Create a climate of trust and confidence where students feel comfortable expressing their opinions.
2 Feedback dialogues seem to work best where there is a task to give the dialogue a structure and a goal.
3 You will need to be very objective throughout the dialogue. When students criticise it can be hard not to become defensive or even aggressive, but it is important that you adopt an accepting attitude. For your students this is their time to say what they liked/didn't like and what they found useful/didn't find useful. Each person's experiences will be different, so this also gives them the opportunity to find out the views of other people in the group. It is through hearing these differences of opinion that the group learns tolerance.
4 In some cases, give students the choice of anonymous feedback. This will depend largely on the level of trust they have, not necessarily in you, but in, for example, the institution where the classes take place.
5 There must be evidence in the days which follow a feedback session that some of their suggestions are being taken on board. Having feedback dialogues, however, doesn't mean that you have to fulfill all the wishes and desires expressed. It is important that you indicate that you have heard and understood everyone's point of view.

FORMAL FEEDBACK DIALOGUES

We generally hold a formal feedback dialogue every twelve to twenty hours, depending on the length of the course. The procedure is:
1 Give everyone an individual written task to do in which they think about what they are doing in class.
2 Students compare with one another what they have written.
3 Students discuss their own impressions and those they have heard others express and have found thought-provoking.
4 You summarise as objectively as you can what has been said and ask students to leave their written feedback papers behind at the end of the class. Once again, make it clear that these papers can be left anonymously.

One such individual written task is 'The Feel Wheel' (Moskowitz 1978, pp. 103–105).

Procedure

1 Ask students to draw a wheel and divide it into four parts like the one in Fig. 4.
2 Tell them to write in their wheel four 'emotions' they are feeling at the moment in relation to their class. For example:

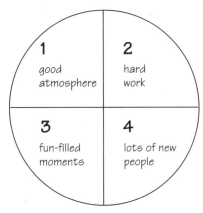

Fig. 4

3 Next, for each emotion they write a sentence explaining why they are experiencing that particular feeling.
4 Students mingle and note any similarities or differences.
5 Bring the group back together and ask each person to share one part of their feel wheel with the whole group.

INFORMAL FEEDBACK DIALOGUES

Business people very often like to review what they are doing and the reasons why. Short ten to fifteen minute feedback sessions held at the end of each lesson help students to take stock of what they have done in class. These sessions are especially important when you are using a communicative activity based approach. Otherwise students may have the feeling that they are going nowhere in particular. A short activity like THE LIST can clear up any misunderstanding about what the point of the lesson was.

1.5

THE LIST

1 Ask students, working individually, to write out a list of everything they did during the lesson.
2 Go over the lists quickly with the group, making sure they are complete and that the reason for doing each activity is clear.
3 Invite each student to say which activities they found the most and the least useful to them personally.

VARIATION
At Step 3, students say which activity they'd like to repeat.

ONE-TO-ONE
After Step 1, students rank the items on their list according to usefulness or some other criterion (e.g. memorability).

1.6

KEEPING DIARIES

Mario Rinvolucri introduced us to the idea of suggesting to students that they keep a diary about their English class. This is quite compatible with teaching business and professional people as they are often asked to write up reports and accounts of business trips and customer contacts. There are no rules for writing these diaries. Students can write them at home or in class as part of their informal feedback dialogue. Some students write their diaries in narrative form while others describe what went on in class. Still others express their own feelings and opinions more personally. Students can, if they wish, share elements of what they have written with each other. Many of our students enjoy reading passages of their diaries to each other.

In one-to-one courses you can establish a running correspondence with your student. This can be initiated by you while the student is doing something else in class, or you can ask the student to write you a letter about the class at home. (For more on this area see Murphey, 1991.)

CHAPTER 2

Presenting information

The activities contained in this chapter give practice in the oral skills people need to make presentations, speak during meetings and symposiums, and function in everyday conversational situations. The focus is on building students' fluency and confidence by helping them to learn these skills first in class and then to progress to their use in the outside world. Consequently, many of these ideas can be used as warm-ups or in the early stages of the group's development when students need to establish contact with each other.

THE INTERVIEW (GROUP VERSION)

This is a good first class activity which gets students talking about what they know well: themselves and their jobs.

Procedure

1 Split the class into interviewers and interviewees and give each student the Idea sheet for their role (see pages 15–16).
2 In pairs, student A interviews student B about B's job. Stress that each interviewer takes notes and should find out as much as possible about the job of the interviewee.
3 After a set time (at least 15 minutes per interview), everyone changes roles (and Idea sheets) and conducts new interviews for the same amount of time.
4 At the end of the second interview, re-form pairs so that each student is with someone that they did not work with before.
5 Re-formed pairs look at the notes they made about their previous partners' jobs and, from these notes, they create and record question-and-answer interviews about the two different jobs. When reconstructing the dialogue, pairs should use first names, ask questions using 'you' and answer using 'I'.
  For example: if (1) Marie and Ana and (2) Jacques and Bruno were the two original pairs, the reshuffled pair of Marie and Jacques will have notes about Ana's and Bruno's jobs. Using their notes, Marie and Jacques create a question-answer dialogue about each job. e.g.
  'Ana, where do you work?'
  'I work in a small international law firm called Brooks and Pearson.'
  'That's interesting; and how long have you worked there?'

2.1

LEVEL
Intermediate+

MATERIALS
Cassette recorders (ideally one for every two students), Idea sheets (see pp. 15–17)

TIME
90 minutes

FOCUS
Asking and answering questions, Information gathering

'I have been with them for almost two years now.'

'And where is your office situated?'

'In the centre of Milano, close to the theatre.'

'How do you use English in your job?'

'I must often type reports for English or American firms that have legal business in Italy.' etc.

6 Re-form the original pairs and let them listen to the reconstructed, recorded dialogues about their own jobs.

7 Bring the group back together and ask students which ideas about their work came across clearly and which were changed or mis-construed. Encourage students to find out why the ideas were not clear: was it a problem of vocabulary, grammar, verb tenses, sentence formation, pronunciation, etc.?

RATIONALE

The twist and interest of this activity comes when the students realise that the recordings are of themselves talking about their jobs.

ACKNOWLEDGEMENT

This activity was inspired by the work of Charles Curran (Curran, 1976).

WORKSHEET FOR ACTIVITIES 2.1 AND 2.2

Ideas for interviewee

1 Before the interview begins look at the following list, think about and write
down notes about different aspects of your job that might be interesting to
the interviewer.

a   organisation of the company

b   organisation of particular departments

c   layout of the plant or building

d   layout of the office

e   special skills or training needed for the job

f   daily routines

g   'atmosphere' in the office

h   colleagues

i   job mobility and possibilities for promotion

j   likes and dislikes about the job

k   advantages and disadvantages of the job

l   pay scale and speed of progression

m   extra benefits or 'perks' such as company cars, company organised holidays, trips, children's holiday camps

n   facilities such as cafeteria, coffee machines, exercise or work-out area,
employee lounge áreas, company sports clubs, libraries and resource
centres

o   on-the-job training programmes or training provided elsewhere

p   transport facilities to and from work

q   job-related travel

r   your own ideas of other aspects you'd like to talk about

2 Listen carefully to the questions you are asked and answer them as completely as possible.

3 Try to be as clear and precise as you can.

4 Be prepared to clarify and expand upon your answers if asked to do so.

WORKSHEET FOR ACTIVITIES 2.1 AND 2.2
Ideas for interviewer

1 Before beginning the interview think about the different aspects of a job (some are mentioned below) and write down questions you can ask in order to find information about each of these aspects from someone who has that job.

a organisation of the company
b organisation of particular departments
c layout of the plant or building
d layout of the office
e special skills or training needed for the job
f daily routines
g 'atmosphere' in the office
h colleagues
i job mobility and possibilities for promotion
j likes and dislikes about the job
k advantages and disadvantages of the job
l pay scale and speed of progression
m extra benefits or 'perks' such as company cars, company organised holidays, trips, children's holiday camps
n facilities such as cafeteria, coffee machines, exercise or work-out area, employee lounge areas, company sports clubs, libraries and resource centres
o on-the-job training programmes or training provided elsewhere
p transport facilities to and from work
q job-related travel
r any other questions you would like to ask (write them here):

2 Use Wh-questions: Who? When? What? Where? Why? and How?
3 Listen carefully to what the interviewee is telling you.
4 Remember that what's important is to get your interviewee to speak, not to speak yourself.
5 Avoid interrupting.
6 Repeat information you are given to help the interviewee clarify or rephrase what has already been said. For example: 'You say you work long hours, what do you mean by long?' or 'You said there are many people in your office, is that right?'
7 Ask questions to get even more information than you have been given. This is useful when the interviewee doesn't seem to know what to say or how to continue. For example: 'You have given me the disadvantages of your job, now can you find any advantages?' or 'What kind of benefits does your company offer its employees?' or 'When must people be present in your office on the flexi-time programme?'

THE INTERVIEW (ONE-TO-ONE)

This activity is a good starting point if you don't know your student's level or needs.

Procedure

STAGE ONE: THE INTERVIEW

1 Explain to your student that you are going to interview them in great detail about their job (or, if they're not working yet, the job they would like to have).
2 Give the student the 'Ideas for interviewee' sheet (see page 15) and give them time to read it over. Check that they understand what they must do.
3 Using the 'Ideas for interviewer' sheet (see page 16), you interview the student and take notes.

STAGE TWO: BETWEEN CLASSES

4 Use your notes to create a question/answer dialogue about the job of your student.
5 With an English-speaking colleague or friend, role play and record this interview, with your friend asking the questions and you taking the role of your student.

STAGE THREE: LISTENING

6 The student listens to the recording and comments on which ideas about their job came across clearly, which were changed or misconstrued and what clarifications or additions could be made.

VARIATIONS

1 With elementary or lower intermediate students you can carry out the interview in their native language and then translate and record it in English. They keep the tape for use as a model.
2 If you have saved a 'library' of previous job descriptions, you may have one from another student with the same type of job as your present student. In this case you can use the recording of an earlier interview in a listening exercise either before or after your present student's interview and playback.
Tasks:
● Listening and noting similar or different points in their job situations.
● Listening and noting points they think are interesting and want to talk about with you.
3 An interview relating to another completely different job description could also be used in the same way as above.
Tasks:
● Listening for similarities and differences in their jobs.
● Listening for ideas about jobs which your student might wish to discuss (for example, good and bad points about the job).

2.2

LEVEL
Elementary+

MATERIALS
Cassette recorder and another English speaker

TIME
Stage one: 30 minutes

Stage two: 30 minutes

Stage three: 30 minutes

FOCUS
Answering questions and giving information

RATIONALE

This activity stimulates students to work on comprehension, because the recording concerns what is most interesting – themselves. For low level students, you can make their first contact with listening to English be about themselves.

2.3

LEVEL
Elementary+

MATERIALS
Paper and various coloured pens

TIME
30 minutes

FOCUS
Organising and presenting personal information

THE CLOCK

This activity gives students, who are perhaps meeting for the first time, the opportunity to find out about each other's careers. In doing this they often find points in common which form a basis for future cooperation.

Procedure

1 Tell students to draw a clock face on a sheet of paper. This represents their past, present and future working life.

   a The hours, minutes and seconds of the clock represent various events or steps in their careers. For example: education, first job, second job, promotion, travel, etc.

   b The number of hours or minutes for each event or step can show either its importance or its length in relation to their career as a whole (see Fig. 5).

   c Lower level students may wish to draw in small pictures or use a few key words only.

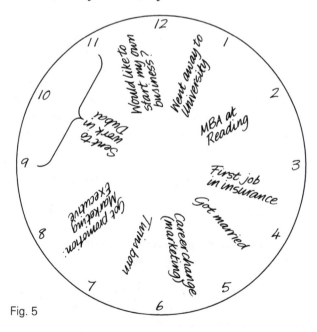

Fig. 5

2 Ask students to form sub-groups of two's or three's and use their clocks as a basis for presenting themselves and their professional lives.

3 Hang the clocks around the room for decoration. Additionally, the clocks on the walls can provide a very real and personal context for later work on tenses. For example, when working the simple past or the present perfect, you can refer to a clock on the wall to contextualise sentences like: 'Pierre changed jobs in 1985' or 'Rosanna has worked at IBM in Rome since 1988'.

COMMENTS

The time spent in drawing the clock gives students time to select and mentally rehearse what they can and wish to say about themselves. You must stress that what's important is speaking about the meaning of the clock, not the artwork involved.

In our experience the most exciting exchanges have come from groups where there is an age difference because the experiences and comparisons are not the same. Perhaps people like looking over the other side of the generation gap!

ONE-TO-ONE

1 You and your student each draw your own clocks as above.

2 Using your clocks, each of you then explains your clock and working life to the other.

ACKNOWLEDGEMENT

THE CLOCK is based on an idea used by museums to help children understand where a particular work of art stands relative to their own lifetime.

WELCOME TO SOBOVIA

This short exercise on presentation technique is very popular with students because it lets them concentrate on their presentation skills without getting bogged down in content. Each presentation is short and interactive so everyone is involved.

Procedure

1 Ask your students to prepare a list of different places to visit in a town or city. Tell them to choose places which will give different impressions of the city, for example, a zoo, a bank, a shopping mall, the town hall, a sports complex, a park, etc. The town can be their own or one related to something they are studying, New York or Oxford for example.

2 Ask students to imagine that they have to work out a guided tour for a visiting foreign delegation. Tell students that the delegation only has one afternoon for this, so they must choose

2.4

LEVEL
Intermediate

MATERIALS
A small blank card for each student, You and Your Audience handout (see below)

TIME
45 minutes (class of six to twelve)

FOCUS
Presentation skills

three places from the list to visit. Each student will become a 'guide' and present the 'three place' tour they have chosen for the delegation.

3 Each two-minute presentation should take the following form:
- Welcome: the presenter comes into the room and welcomes the delegation.
- Introduction: the presenter introduces her/himself and says what they do.
- Presentation of visit: they briefly tell the delegation the places they are going to visit in the city and why.
- Closing: the presenter thanks the delegation and wishes them a good afternoon.

4 Give everyone a small blank card and tell students that they have five minutes to write down speaking notes on their blank card. (The small size of the card stops students trying to write down every word.)

5 Determine an order for the presentations, each student being a 'guide' in turn. The students who are not the 'guide' become 'delegates' and arrange themselves in some kind of order either sitting in rows or standing around the room.

6 The 'guide' goes out and then comes back into the room to make their presentation. (Going out of and coming back into the room is psychologically important because it helps everyone to imagine that each 'guide' is facing a new delegation for the first time.)

7 Students generally like some teacher feedback about their presentations. You can comment on their entrance, ease of delivery or the way they involved the audience, for example.

Opposite is a handout with some ideas which can help participants attract and maintain audience attention during a presentation. You can go over it with your class before they make their presentations to give them some pointers, and then ask them to look at it after their presentations to see which they did or didn't do.

VARIATION
Students present the delegation with a tour of their company instead of a town or city.

ONE-TO-ONE
Follow the same steps as above.

WORKSHEET FOR ACTIVITY 2.4

You and your audience

- Did you attract the audience's attention? For example, 'May I have your attention please?'
- Did you make a reference to the audience themselves? For example, 'It's so nice to have the delegation from Morocco with us today.'
- Did you ask if everyone could hear you clearly and speak up if they could not?
- Did you keep good eye-contact and remember to look at everyone, or did you bury your head in your paper?
- Did you use some gestures or body movement to keep their attention?
- Did you use a visual aid or write something on the board?
- Did you ask them a question and involve your audience? For example, 'Could someone tell me the places we are going to visit?'
- Did you use signposts to help the audience follow your presentation? For example, 'First, we will visit . . .' or 'After that, we will go to the . . .'

2.5

LEVEL
Elementary+

MATERIALS
Identical sheets of
paper

TIME
20 minutes

FOCUS
Asking questions,
Use of the simple
past tense, Tag
questions

MY LAST TRIP

This recipe works well for people who travel for business or pleasure
and for students who need practice using the simple past. It gives
them very concrete personal topics to talk about which make for
lively, interested participation.

Procedure

1 Give each student a sheet of paper and tell them to divide it into six
equal parts; first drawing a vertical line down the middle, then two
horizontal lines.
2 Tell students to write the following things at the bottom of each
block:

upper left-hand corner: Where I went
upper right-hand corner: How I travelled
middle left: Who went with me
middle right: Something I did
lower left-hand corner: Something I brought back
lower right-hand corner: Something I wish I had done

3 Now ask students to quickly and secretly answer these questions
about their last trips in the form of sketches instead of words.
Stress that their artistic ability isn't important, they are only trying
to convey ideas.
4 Collect the papers and display them on the floor or on a table.
5 Following these rules, students ask each other questions to find out
which paper belongs to whom:
  ● Each person in turn asks a question about any of the papers to
  any other student.
  ● Students can ask only 'yes' or 'no' questions.
  ● A 'no' answer passes the turn to another student.
  ● The game is to practise asking and answering questions by
  seeing who can get the longest string of 'yes' answers, so even
  when a student knows whose paper it is they continue to ask
  questions until they lose their turn.
  ● A simple question/answer exchange might go something like
  this:
  'Marisol, did you go to England on your last trip?' 'Yes, I did.'
  'Did you travel by boat?' 'Yes, I did.'
  'Did you travel with your boss?' 'Yes, I did.'
  'Did you visit the Bank of England?' 'Yes, I did.'
  'Did you bring back toys for your children?' 'Yes, I did.'
  'Do you wish you had visited the Tower of London?' 'Yes, I do.'

VARIATION

In higher level classes, once the students know which paper belongs to whom, students ask tag questions to verify the rest of the information in the different pictures. The same dialogue might then go something like this:

'Marisol, did you go to England on your last trip?' 'Yes, I did.'

'Did you travel by boat?' 'Yes, I did.'

'Oh, you travelled with your boss, didn't you?' 'Yes, I did.'

'And you visited the Bank of England, didn't you?' 'Yes, I did.'

'So you brought back toys for your children?' 'Yes, I did.'

'And you would have liked to visit the Tower of London; is that right?' 'Yes, I would.'

THE SPEECH

This activity introduces students step by step to different components of successful public speaking: entrance, attitude, intonation, volume and rapidity of speech, and body language.

Procedure

STAGE ONE: ENTRANCE

1 Divide your class into two groups. The first group practises coming into a room in the following ways:
   - taking small steps/large steps
   - as noisily/as quietly as possible
   - full of self-confidence/lacking in self-confidence
   - aware of others in the room/totally unaware of anyone else's presence
   - ready and prepared to speak publicly/absolutely unprepared
   - with a positive attitude/with a negative attitude

   The second group is the audience and observes the entrances.
2 Groups reverse roles and repeat the entrances.

STAGE TWO: READING THE SPEECH

3 Give each student a copy of the speech (see page 24).
4 Pair students and ask them to work together on the speech doing the following:
   ● Reading it through silently for the sense of the words, deciding where full stops and commas should go and putting them in.
   ● Reading the speech out loud, pausing for the commas and full stops.
   ● Working on variations in intonation: first reading as flatly as possible, then with as much exaggeration as possible, and finally finding a natural intonation in the middle.
   ● Working on changes in volume: reading as softly as possible, then as loudly, and finding a comfortable volume in the middle.

2.6

LEVEL
Intermediate

MATERIALS
A photocopy of The Speech for each student (see below)

TIME
30 minutes

FOCUS
Public speaking skills

- Working on speed: reading as slowly and as fast as possible.
- Working on variations of body language using the attitudes practised in Stage One: confident, nervous, self-conscious, etc.

STAGE THREE: GIVING THE SPEECH

5 Students take turns delivering their speeches, combining the elements worked on above: entrance, attitude, intonation, volume, speed, and body language.

6 The rest of the group acts as the audience.

COMMENT

The speech appears in capital letters to give students the opportunity to punctuate as they wish.

ONE-TO-ONE

1 Record the intonation work done during Stage Two on a cassette recorder.

2 Video the work done on body language during Stage one and the final presentation in Stage Three.

The speech

FIRST OF ALL I'D LIKE TO SAY HOW PLEASED I AM TO BE HERE TODAY WHAT I AM GOING TO SAY CONCERNS US ALL EVERY SINGLE ONE OF US NO MATTER WHAT OUR POSITION THERE ARE FOUR THOUSAND MILLION MEN WOMEN AND CHILDREN ON OUR LITTLE PLANET ALL OF US ARE STRUGGLING FROM DAY TO DAY SOME FOR THEIR FOOD OTHERS FOR THEIR FREEDOM HERE IN THIS COUNTRY WE ARE STRUGGLING TOGETHER TO PRESERVE A WAY OF LIFE THAT IS VERY DEAR TO US ALL I'D LIKE TO SAY WHAT WE SHOULD DO IT'S NOT THEORIES THAT COUNT IT'S PRACTICE

(*All's Well 2* (Dickinson, Leveque, Sagot, 1976) Language Games, Unit Seven.)

THE EXECUTIVE PARKING LOT

This activity is not for all groups, but engineers and technicians particularly enjoy problem-solving. Here we take problem-solving a step further and challenge students' language abilities and presentation skills by asking them to explain exactly how they reached their solutions.

Procedure

1 Divide your class into pairs or groups of three or four (see page 27).
2 Give each group a copy of the problem sheet.
3 Go over the problem with the groups. Point out that there are five different cars and each has six distinctive characteristics.
4 Give the groups five minutes to read, understand, and organise the information in the first seven statements in grid form. We usually let our students work out a grid form for themselves but if they really get stuck you can give them the sample one below (Fig. 6) to help them.

		Far left	Left	Middle	Right	Far right
Company's Nationality	GERMAN	X	X	✓	X	X
	JAPANESE			X		
	AMERICAN			X		
	ITALIAN			X		
	?			X		
Emblem	JAGUAR	✓	X	X	X	X
	HORSE	X				
	?	X				
	?	X				
	?	X				

Fig. 6

5 Tell them to answer the first question. Go around and help groups with any vocabulary in the problem that they might not know.
6 Ask a volunteer to come up to the board and draw the table.
7 Call on another student to put a piece of information into the table, asking them to explain with very precise language exactly how they reached the conclusion that the piece of information they have chosen belongs there.
8 Each student in turn places a fact in the table and explains the reasoning behind their conclusions.
9 Continue in this way through the first seven statements until they have all found the answer to the first question.
10 Groups re-form and work on the last seven statements for another five minutes, explaining their logic to each other.
11 Students come to the board one by one and do as in Step 7 above until they all find the answer to the second question and solve the problem. (See Fig. 7.)

2.7

LEVEL
Intermediate+

MATERIALS
A photocopy of The Executive Parking Lot problem sheet for each group of students (see below)

TIME
30 minutes

FOCUS
Problem-solving and presentation skills

ANSWER TABLE – THE EXECUTIVE PARKING LOT

Car's position	FAR LEFT	LEFT	MIDDLE	RIGHT	FAR RIGHT
Company's Nationality	BRITISH	ITALIAN	GERMAN	AMERICAN	JAPANESE
Emblem	JAGUAR	HORSE	STAR	CROSS	LION
Car design	FOUR-DOOR	TWO-DOOR	FIVE-DOOR	SLIDING DOOR	THREE-DOOR
Characteristics	SEDAN	CONVERTIBLE	STATION WAGON	VAN	HATCHBACK
Executive's language	ENGLISH	ITALIAN	DUTCH	SPANISH	FRENCH
Car colour	SILVER	RED	WHITE	NAVY BLUE AND TAN	GREEN AND WHITE

Fig. 7

COMMENT

Be careful to point out the difference between facts and assumptions. For example, a student may assume that the executive of the Japanese company is Japanese, but this is an assumption and not a proven fact. The table can only hold proven facts.

ONE-TO-ONE

As above, but with the student presenting to you.

With lower level students you can present the first few sentences for them in order to model the precise language you want them to use.

WORKSHEETS FOR ACTIVITY 2.7

The executive parking lot

My company was a multinational conglomerate but I hadn't really realised it until one day I gazed out the window and noticed the executives' cars in the parking lot. There was an important meeting that day and the five differently coloured cars directly below my window all belonged to executives working for companies of different nationalities based in those different countries. Each car had an emblem on its hood and none of the cars had the same design characteristics. I knew that the executive owners of each car all spoke different languages.

1 The company whose executive owns the car in the middle is German.
2 The car on the far left has a jaguar emblem.
3 The two-door convertible is next to the car with a jaguar on the hood.
4 The three-door hatchback is just to the right of the van with the sliding doors (sporting American licence plates from California).
5 The executive of the American company is a native speaker of Spanish.
6 The three-door hatchback has Japanese registration.
7 The car with a rearing horse emblem belongs to an Italian company.

Now can you answer this question? WHICH MAKE OF CAR BELONGS TO THE EXECUTIVE WHO WORKS FOR THE BRITISH COMPANY AND WHERE IS IT POSITIONED?

8 The five-door station wagon has a star on its hood.
9 The owner of the four-door sedan is English-speaking.
10 Next to the red convertible is the four-door sedan.
11 The car with the lion emblem has an owner who speaks French.
12 The car with a flattened cross emblem is navy blue and tan.
13 The Dutch-speaking executive's car is white.
14 The Italian-speaking executive's car is parked next to the silver one.

Now can you answer this question? WHICH OF THE CARS IS GREEN AND WHITE?

2.8

LEVEL
Intermediate

MATERIALS
A short (2–3
minute maximum)
video clip of a
newsreader
presenting a
commentary, An
unpunctuated
script of the
commentary

TIME
30 minutes

FOCUS
Coordination of
breathing,
gestures, facial
expression and
the spoken word

NEWS PLAYBACK

'News playback' presents a method of working on the skill of reading out loud. It involves the student in matching their breathing, gestures and facial expressions to those of a professional newsreader. This activity concentrates on improving non-linguistic skills for a more natural and fluent oral presentation.

Procedure

1 Play the video clip and ask the students to observe the breathing of the newsreader. The clue to doing this is to listen for pauses, no matter how brief.

2 Show the film to the class a second time. Ask students to indicate each time the newsreader pauses by knocking on the table.

3 Play the clip a third time, ask students to coordinate their breathing with the newsreader's. To do this tell them to hold their breath while the reader is speaking and to breathe in or out during the pauses.

4 Stop here for an awareness-raising discussion. Ask students what clues they have been using to gauge their breathing – visual clues, words, stress patterns, or something else?

5 Tell them to observe the head and hand gestures of the newsreader, looking for correlations between a particular word or phrase and a gesture. Play the clip again.

6 Ask students to imagine they are a mirror in front of the newsreader. They reflect back all the head or hand movements they see. Play the clip again.

7 Next, students imitate facial expressions and, if there are any, body movements or changes in attitude or position, such as shifts to the right or left, leaning forwards or backwards.

8 Ask students to put it all together by imitating the newsreader's breathing, pauses, gestures, facial expressions and body language. Show the clip at least once more.

9 Video students role playing the newsreader with the sound of the news commentary in the background.

10 The class watches the film to see themselves reading the news as naturally as a native speaker.

COMMENT

Give your students a copy of the transcript if you think this will help them feel more relaxed during the imitation work.

Take special care to keep up the pace and rhythm of this activity so that students don't lose interest.

ACKNOWLEDGEMENT
We saw this technique demonstrated at Pilgrims in Canterbury, England in August, 1990 by David Larbalestier.

CHOOSING A COMPANY NAME

This exercise can be used as an opener in a business course to get students thinking about businesses and the images projected by their names.

Procedure

1 Put students in groups of four or less.
2 Give each group a photocopy of the list of company names and the five tasks to do with these names. Set a time limit of twenty minutes.
3 After the time limit is up, create new groups with one or two from one group joining one or two from another and ask them to compare their ideas.

ACKNOWLEDGEMENT
This exercise comes from Gerry Kenny.

Choosing a company name

TECHNUM
IF TECH
MARK TECH
IMPULSION
OPTIMUS
INNOVUM
NOVENA
TECHLANCE
TECHTRAILS
TECHWAYS
PYRAMID

1 In your opinon, which are the three best names for a technically innovative company? Why?
2 Which name do you consider the least appropriate for this kind of high tech company? Why?
3 What sort of product or service does the name INNOVUM Inc. suggest to you?
4 Choose one of the names from the above list and describe the company and its products or services.
5 Invent a letterhead and/or a logo for one of the companies from the list.

2.9

LEVEL
Intermediate+

MATERIALS
A photocopy of several ideas for a company name for each group (see below)

TIME
30 minutes

FOCUS
Decision making and discussing

2.10

LEVEL
Intermediate+

MATERIALS
One blank card
per student

TIME
20 minutes for a
class of six

FOCUS
Formal
introductions
before an
audience

LET ME INTRODUCE

Through practice in introducing people and being introduced in front of a group, this activity builds up student confidence about speaking in public and makes them aware of aspects of their behaviour before a group.

Procedure

1 Elicit or teach introductory phrases such as the following:
   Let me introduce . . .
   It's my pleasure to present . . .
   This is . . .
   It's my great honour to present my distinguished colleague . . .
2 Ask students to rank these in order of formality.
   For example: 'It's an honour to introduce my distinguished colleague . . .' is more formal than 'Let me introduce . . .'.
3 Tell students to take notes as you orally present the following dos and don'ts:
   ● Don't speak until you are actually in front of the audience – not while walking across the room.
   ● Speak loudly and clearly enough so that the person in the last row can hear you.
   ● Maintain eye contact with the audience, not with the written card.
   ● Avoid unnecessary foot movements – no dancing and shuffling around. This will distract from the message.
   ● Be aware of what you do with your hands – avoid hand-wringing and fiddling with fingernails or small objects.
4 Give out the blank cards. Ask each student to write their name, their job and a project they are working on. This may be real or, if your students aren't working, imaginary. Something like this:

   Francis Tsai
   Director, INSEE
   Coordinating the census for the south-west of France

   Dagelbert Dodo
   President of the Interplanetary Commission
   Negotiating for world peace

5 Collect cards, then redistribute them so that noone has their own.
6 Tell your students they are going to introduce the person whose card they have before a real audience. Give them a few minutes to jot down a few key words to make their introductions.
7 Arrange the class like an audience. This is very important in motivating good, realistic delivery.

8 Ask one student to start off. They step out of the room, re-enter, make their introduction and ask the person they have introduced to please stand up. Continue until everyone has introduced someone.

9 Encourage the audience to respond to each introduction by clapping.

10 Conduct a feedback session with reference to the dos and don'ts mentioned during Step 3.

11 If you have access to a video camera and your students are used to being filmed, this is a good activity to film for viewing and feedback. You or the 'audience' can award points from one to three to each student for their introduction, based on the dos and don'ts.

ONE-TO-ONE
You and your student introduce each other.

If possible, arrange to do this in front of another class. Prepare cards about each other but with more information than in the group version. For example: home town or city / nationality / age / married / children / other personal information.

RATIONALE
We do this activity with most groups of business people because, although it is short and simple, it gives them good feedback on their ability to communicate effectively in public. By preparing to speak successfully before an audience, students build up confidence in themselves.

NOTE
In one lower intermediate class, the 'audience' wore cartoon character masks during the introductions. The speakers said this made them feel more at ease!

2.11

LEVEL
Intermediate+

MATERIAL
Maps of about ten
countries

TIME
45 minutes

FOCUS
Listening,
Expressing
opinions,
Agreeing/
Disagreeing

PAST EXPERIENCES / FUTURE PLANS

This is a good activity for students who have lived abroad or who
would like to live abroad. In groups where some people have lived in
a foreign country while others haven't, dreams and reality can meet,
with exciting results.

Preparation

1 Find maps of about ten countries; photocopy and enlarge them.
You need a thoroughly diverse selection, for example: Scotland,
South Africa, New Zealand, Texas, USA, Egypt, Japan, Iraq, Saudi
Arabia, Cuba.
2 Place the maps on the wall around the classroom.

Procedure

1 Tell the class about an experience you or someone you know has
had living abroad. Elicit further stories from the group.
2 Explain that they are going to have the chance to live and work
abroad for a few years and that jobs are available in the countries
they see around the room.
3 Invite everyone to take pen and paper and walk around, ranking the
countries in order of preference and noting down pros and cons
about living and working in each.
For example (Fig. 8):

*Iraq-number 9
An interesting country historically
Cheap
Good pay
Hard for women
Not much to do
Dangerous political situation*

Fig. 8

4 Bring the group back together. Poll your class to see which country
had the most votes for place number one. Discuss pros and cons.
5 Continue through the list in this way until you work through all the
countries.

ACKNOWLEDGEMENT
This activity is based on an idea used by Paul Harlow.

WORKSPACES

If yours is an in-company course, this activity can lead to action if the company takes account of students' wishes. If not, it at least gives students a chance to think again about an often forgotten aspect of an employee's well-being, the environment in which they work. Any workspace is suitable – office, workshop, classroom, etc.

Procedure

1 Brainstorm the qualities found in the ideal workspace. Ask a student to write these on the board.
2 Put students in small groups and ask them to find ways of classifying these qualities.
3 Each group reports their classification to the whole class.
4 Ask students to each take a sheet of paper and some felt pens and draw their ideal workspace.
5 When they finish, they each write three adjectives describing their workspace at the top of their sketch.
6 Either: invite the group to move around and mingle and compare their sketches. Or: set up an exhibition of the sketches and as the group moves around from sketch to sketch each student comments on their own.
7 Bring the group back together for a pooling session entitled 'I noticed . . .' in which they list what they have noticed about the sketches. Keep this phase moving quickly.

ONE-TO-ONE
1 You and your student each have three minutes to interview the other around the theme of 'what is important to me in a workspace'.
2 You design your ideal workspaces and present them to each other.

2.12

LEVEL
Intermediate+

MATERIAL
Large pieces of white drawing paper, several coloured felt pens per student

TIME
30 minutes

FOCUS
Describing a work area, Discussion/ Problem-solving

2.13

LEVEL
Elementary

MATERIALS
A photocopy of
Remember my
Name worksheet
for each student
(see below)

TIME
15 minutes

FOCUS
Practise
pronouncing
English names
and jobs

REMEMBER MY NAME

Learning and remembering names is often a problem for all of us, but especially for students of a foreign language. This activity gives students practice in pronouncing English names and common jobs. It also aims at enhancing students' ability to remember names, a skill which they will find useful in their professional lives.

Procedure

1 Hand out copies of the worksheet below. (When you are familiar with this activity, you might want to make up a list of your own.)
2 Start by saying that the students have to work out the logical connection between the people and their jobs. For example, William Thompson is a technician and Frank Darrison is a director. Give students a few moments to think about this.
3 Ask a student what Sandy Stevenson is. If the student says he's a supervisor or a salesman, say that this is correct (any job beginning with a different letter is wrong) and ask another student what Peter Billings is. They should say he's a banker or some other job beginning with 'b'.
4 Keep going around the class asking students what different people on the list do until you're sure everyone has caught on that the name of the person and their job should begin with the same letter. Then ask one student to explain the rule.
5 Now change the rule and say that Anne Albers is a banker. Next ask a student what Frank Darrison is. He's an accountant, right? The surname and the job have the same number of syllables. Go around the room again until you're sure everyone has caught on. Then ask one student to explain the rule.
6 Give the game over to your students and let them find a rule for putting the names and jobs together. Tell them they don't have to match *all* of the jobs with *all* of the names. This will almost certainly not be possible!

VARIATIONS
a The job noun starts with the last letter of the first name or surname.
b The job noun has one more or one less letter than the first name or surname.
Have fun!

ONE-TO-ONE
All these games can be played one-to-one. Don't forget to ask the student to explain what the connection is.

A variation for one-to-one is to do this exercise over the telephone (for telephone listening practice).

COMMENT
Interestingly, experiments have shown that it's easier to remember people by their jobs than by their names. You might ask students if

they have noticed this. In the past, names typically described occupations – in fact, Mason, Butcher, Carpenter and so on are still common names. A good tip to give your students could be to try and always tell people what their jobs are – they might be remembered more easily! Ask students if they have any techniques for remembering names.

WORKSHEET FOR ACTIVITY 2.13

Remember my name

JOBS	NAMES
technician	Fiona Evanston-Jones
manager	Peter Billings
postman	Thomas Smith
electrician	Clive Peterson
clerk	Archibald Cunningham
supervisor	Marsha Emery
factory worker	Sam Miller
accountant	Anne Albers
banker	Frank Darrison
administrator	Jim Taylor-Steadman
director	Sandy Stevenson
teacher	Bruce Falkensmitherson
engineer	Patricia Adamson-Collins
salesman	William Thompson

2.14

Intermediate+

MATERIALS
A Guide Sheet or
Checklist for each
student (see
below)

TIME
60 minutes

FOCUS
Asking/
responding to
questions,
Gathering
information,
Reformulating and
clarifying
information

THE JOB INTERVIEW

This activity gives students specialised training in asking and answering questions in a job interview. This is especially useful for students in business schools, for people who will have job interviews in English or for personnel managers who interview people.

Procedure

1 Ask the class to make a list of about ten unusual or funny jobs. For example, a lion-tamer in a circus, a Hollywood stunt man, a personal maid to the Queen of England, a writer for soap opera dialogue, etc.

2 Give a copy of either the Interviewer's Guide Sheet or the Interviewee's Guide Sheet or the Observer's Checklist to each student (see pages 37–39).

3 Form groups of three: an interviewer, an interviewee who is qualified for and wants the job, and an observer who will listen to the interview and take notes on their checklist.

4 Tell each group of three they have ten minutes to individually prepare a job interview for one of the jobs on the class list. During this preparation period you move around the room and help out with language problems.

5 Allow ten minutes for the first round of interviews. At the end of these interviews, the observer has five minutes to report back observations.

6 Students in each threesome change roles and they continue with a second and third round of interviews and feedback as above until each student has taken each role. During the second and third round, groups should choose different jobs from the class list.

NOTE
Be prepared to explain the use of *they/their* (on the Observer's Checklist and Interviewer's Guide Sheet) to refer to a single person without specifying sex.

WORKSHEETS FOR ACTIVITIES 2.14 AND 2.15

Interviewer's guide sheet

1 You are going to interview someone for a job. Make a list of information about the different aspects of the job which you will need to discuss with them. Here are some ideas:
   - organisation of the company
   - organisation of particular departments
   - physical work environment
   - daily routines
   - special skills/abilities and training necessary for the job
   - job profile (what exactly are the tasks and responsibilities of this job?)

2 Make a second list of questions you will ask the interviewee to check their suitability for this job. For example:
   - previous employment
   - special skills
   - attitudes towards work and colleagues
   - why they want this job
   - why they think they are qualified for it

3 Ask the interviewee questions to see what kind of job they are looking for. What are their main criteria for a job?

4 Try to vary questions between more open and closed ones. Closed questions can be answered by only 'yes' or 'no', but open questions require the interviewee to provide more information.

5 Ask questions to get even more information than you have got so far. For example: 'You say you worked in a team in your last job. Could you describe that team to me, especially your part in it?'

6 Think about how to begin and end your interview. You could begin like this: 'Good morning/afternoon. My name is Jean Dupont, and I am in charge of human resources here. I'd like to ask you a few questions.'

WORKSHEET FOR ACTIVITIES 2.14 AND 2.15

Interviewee's guide sheet

1 You are going to be interviewed for a job. Make a list of questions you would ask to find out information about different aspects of the job. Here are some ideas:
   – organisation of the company
   – organisation of particular departments
   – physical work environment
   – daily routines
   – special skills/abilities and training necessary for the job
   – job profile (what exactly are the tasks and responsibilities of this job?)
2 Make a second list of your qualifications and experience which prove your suitability for this job. For example:
   – previous employment
   – special skills
   – attitudes towards work and colleagues
   – why you want this job
   – why you think you are qualified for it
3 Think about how to begin and end your interview. You could begin like this:
   'Good morning/afternoon. I'm Paul Peterson from Birmingham and I've come for an interview about the position as a lion-tamer in your circus.'

WORKSHEET FOR ACTIVITIES 2.14 AND 2.15

Observer's checklist

Observing the interviewer

1 What was the attitude of the interviewer towards the interviewee?

  – Did they introduce themselves?

  – Did they put the interviewee at ease by asking a few friendly questions?

2 Was their presentation of the job clear and precise?

3 Were their questions for the interviewee appropriate in relation to the job?

4 Was there progression and variation in the different types of questions?

  Note down a closed question you heard (answered by yes or no).

  Note down an open question you heard (looking for information).

5 How did the interviewer close the interview?

Observing the interviewee

1 Were they relaxed and at ease during the interview?

2 Did they answer the questions they were asked?

3 Were their answers clear?

4 Did they ask for more detailed or precise information about the job?

5 Did they convince the interviewer that they would be good for the job?

© Longman Group Ltd. 1995 Photocopiable

2.15

LEVEL
Elementary+

MATERIALS
Paper plates,
different kinds of
paper, elastic or
shoe strings to
attach the masks,
coloured felt
pens, and other
decorative bits
and pieces

TIME
45 minutes to
make a mask

30 minutes per
activity

FOCUS
Oral fluency,
Situational
language

MASKS

In role plays, teachers often tell students, 'imagine you are someone', or 'pretend you're in the 1960s' or 'at the grocer's', etc. But for many students, this is too open and lacking in direction. What they need is a strategy applicable in any situation and which provides a structure that stimulates them to speak.

In this set of activities students each make a mask which represents a character they would like to play. (We always give students a choice between attaching their masks or holding them up.)

How do business people react to making masks? In our experience the masks are a powerful aid to concentration and, additionally, reduce anxiety. Even lower level students find rich and unexpected things to say from behind a mask. The key lies in your attitude: if you feel comfortable asking them to make and use masks, they find the work enjoyable, relaxing and enriching. Masks seem to work best with students who are reluctant to do traditional role plays because they are timid or feel they have no acting ability.

Preparation

Bring the materials for making the masks to class, or tell your students in advance that they are going to make masks and ask them to bring materials.

Procedure

1 Students create their own clearly defined characters by deciding details under the following headings:

name	hobbies and interests
age	family
nationality	friends
profession	physical appearance

2 Invite students to take whatever mask-making materials they want to use and allow them thirty minutes to make their masks. Suggest they work in pairs to help each other put the eyeholes in their masks.

3 Tell students to keep the following points in mind when using the masks:
   - Students speak on behalf of their character. This means all questions are in the second person and all answers in the first person.
   - Everyone should wear or hold up a mask during the activities to contribute to the success.

4 The following activities can be created around the finished masks:

A INTRODUCTIONS

- Let me Introduce. (2.10) Students can introduce their mask character and then don their masks (or vice versa!).
- Organise a cocktail party where students mingle. This is especially effective for in-company classes where they already know each other; using masks adds a new dimension and students don't feel silly asking questions they already know the answer to.

B INTERVIEWS AND QUESTIONNAIRES

- The Job Interview. (2.14)
- Journalistic interviews.
- A police interrogation.
- Questionnaires about daily routines, likes and dislikes, etc. Students feel less intimidated when asking and answering questions from behind a mask. We've observed that students are more truthful about themselves when they answer as if they were someone else.

C DESCRIPTIONS

Students describe these things as seen through their masks: workspaces, homes, neighbourhoods, themselves, family, friends.

D ROLE PLAYS

- Students read a dialogue in their coursebook as their character.
- Two or three masked characters create a dialogue for themselves and act it out.
- Organise a business meeting with the characters as participants.
- Have characters negotiate the sale of their homes or cars with each other.

VARIATION

For short, intensive courses where class-time is at a premium, use store bought face masks, hats, or faces drawn on balloons.

Students can also swap masks and, looking at the world through new eyes, do or redo any of the above activities.

ONE-TO-ONE

Masks are especially useful in one-to-one work because they provide the class with new characters, thus creating a breathing space for the teacher and student.

One student in a one-to-one class made a mask and cut out and pasted on it magazine pictures of half a dozen different people who all became a part of his lesson.

2.16

LEVEL
Intermediate

MATERIALS
Chairs in groups
of three

TIME
30 minutes

FOCUS
Listening and
speaking,
Asking/answering
questions

BOSS OR COLLEAGUE

This activity involves describing people and then role playing them. Assuming the role of a person you know is a powerful way of gaining insight into what makes that person tick. It is a useful technique to use with students before interviews, business meetings, or negotiations. During role plays with business people, we often concentrate on a boss or colleague, but students can choose any person they know well for their description and role play.

Preparation

Arrange chairs in separate groups of three set as far apart as possible. This is vital for the success of this role play so that students experience a feeling of intimacy or privacy.

Procedure

STAGE ONE

1 Ask students to sit in pairs. Next to each pair is an empty chair.
2 Ask everyone to think of a boss or a colleague that they have had. You may want to speak about a boss or colleague of your own to get the exercise going.
3 Tell students to draw the silhouette of this person and inside each silhouette write down any words they associate with this person.
4 Student A tells B about their silhouetted boss or colleague.
5 Student B listens without interrupting and then echoes back to A what they heard without adding or changing anything.
6 Switch roles and repeat Steps 4 and 5 above.

STAGE TWO

7 Student A places their silhouette on the empty chair and agrees to speak on behalf of that person.
8 Student B addresses the silhouette on the chair and asks any questions they wish. Questions must be asked in the second person.
9 Student A answers the questions in the first person using *I*. A's answers at all times should be in role.
10 Eye contact for A and B should be directed towards the chair at all times.
11 A and B change roles and repeat Steps 7 to 10 above.

ONE-TO-ONE
Same as above.

RATIONALE
Empty chair role plays are very useful and good fun when teaching one-to-one. They allow you and your student to 'invite' countless guests into the classroom.

ACKNOWLEDGEMENT
Empty chair role plays are used extensively in Psychodramaturgie Linguistique. We have seen Bernard and Marie Dufeu (University of Mainz) use this technique often. For variations as well as for suggestions for further reading, see John Morgan's empty chair role plays (in Lindstromberg 1990, pp. 42–43, 45–46).

CHAPTER 3

Business communication on the phone

The purpose of these activities is to develop telephone competence. Over and over again students tell us that speaking on the telephone is one of the most demanding things asked of them in their daily professional lives. Why is this? Many people suffer from telephone anxiety; they simply don't like speaking on the phone in any situation and especially in a foreign language. There is often a feeling of being invaded when the phone rings unexpectedly and someone asks for information or asks questions they don't have ready answers to. It's so tempting to ask someone else who's apparently more at ease on the phone to make that outgoing call! Our activities on incoming and outgoing calls help students to develop strategies for communicating by telephone. Through awareness of these strategies and with practice, telephoning becomes a welcome challenge they feel prepared for. These stimulating and fun telephone activities can be done inside or outside the classroom. They help students to get over the difficulties of using the telephone in English and, as their anxiety decreases, their ability to be a successful telephone user grows.

3.1

LEVEL
Beginner+

MATERIALS
Photocopies of the Alphabet Games Sheet

TIME
20 minutes

FOCUS
Spelling out loud, Pronunciation

ALPHABET GAMES

Here are a few ideas for games to make alphabet and spelling practice a bit of fun. Spelling is an important skill for students who use the telephone, as spelling a word is their last chance if they can't make themselves understood any other way.

Procedure

1 Give everybody a photocopy of the Alphabet Games sheet (see page 46).
2 Model the pronunciation of each letter of the alphabet and ask students to repeat. Then vary your intonation and ask students to do the same. Finally, practise the pronunciation of the letters in different ways, for example:
  ● Ask each student to choose a letter they like the sound of and say it out loud.
  ● Then ask them to say one they dislike.

- Continue with one they find easy to say and one they find difficult.
- Ask them to choose a letter in their first name and say it in the way they feel about their name.

3 In the same way, model the pronunciation of the first names on the Alphabet Games sheet. Then practise pronunciation and spelling in various ways, for example:
  - Ask each student in turn to choose a name and spell it out loud. The others listen and call out the name.
  - Writing on backs: Pair students with student A standing behind B. Student A chooses a name and, using a finger, writes it out letter by letter on B's back. Student B says each letter as he or she recognises it.

4 Ask students in pairs to spell out names using the International Aviation Alphabet. For example: Student A: 'E as in *echo*, D as in *delta*, W as in *whisky*, A as in *alpha*, R as in *Romeo*, and D as in *delta*.' Student B: 'That spells *Edward*.'

5 In plenary, students brainstorm different categories they could use to make their own 'alphabets'. For example: animals (*anteater*, *beaver*, *condor*, etc.); fruits and vegetables (*apple*, *beet*, *carrot*, etc.); articles of clothing; furniture; office objects; famous people; things to eat, etc.

6 In groups of three or four, students choose a category and create an alphabet and fill in their sheets.

7 Groups show their alphabets to each other and help other groups to fill in any missing words.

ONE-TO-ONE
Same as above.

VARIATION
Students use the Morse code to practise the alphabet.

WORKSHEET FOR ACTIVITY 3.1
Alphabet games

LETTER	INTERNATIONAL AVIATION	NAME	MORSE CODE	YOURS
A	ALPHA	ALEXANDER	. —	....
B	BRAVO	BENJAMIN	— . . .	....
C	CHARLIE	CHARLES	— . — .	....
D	DELTA	DONALD	— . .	....
E	ECHO	EDWARD	.	....
F	FOXTROT	FRANK	. . — .	....
G	GOLF	GEORGE	— — .	....
H	HOTEL	HENRY	. . . .	....
I	INDIA	ISOBEL	. .	....
J	JULIET	JAMES	. — — —	....
K	KILO	KATHERINE	— . —	....
L	LIMA	LUKE	. — . .	....
M	MIKE	MARY	— —	....
N	NOVEMBER	NANCY	— .	....
O	OSCAR	OLIVER	— — —	....
P	PAPA	PETER	. — — .	....
Q	QUEBEC	QUENTIN	— — . —	....
R	ROMEO	ROBERT	. — .	....
S	SIERRA	STEVE	. . .	....
T	TANGO	TOMMY	—	....
U	UNIFORM	ULYSSES	. . —	....
V	VICTOR	VERONICA	. . . —	....
W	WHISKY	WILLIAM	. — —	....
X	X-RAY	XAVIER	— . . —	....
Y	YANKEE	YORK	— . — —	....
Z	ZULU	ZOE	— — . .	....

CIRCLE INTONATION

On the telephone, business names might well be the first thing a caller hears. Below, we have provided a list of business names containing sounds which foreign learners often find difficult to pronounce and understand. The technique used here to practise intonation is one of our favourites because it gives the initiative to the students.

Procedure

1 Write on the board the list of names provided below (or make up your own list).
2 Ask the group to stand or sit in a circle. It is important that everyone can see the board and that you have room to stand behind each student. (You will move around from student to student and lay a hand gently on each shoulder to signal that it is their turn.)
3 When you signal their turn, students call out the number of a name on the list that they would like you to pronounce.
4 Say the name with natural stress, rhythm and intonation.
5 Tell your student to echo back the name as they hear you say it. Vary intonation, stress, volume and speed each time you say the name. Explain that you will continue saying the name for as long as they wish to repeat after you. The student echoes back what they hear you say after each repetition. They tell you when they want to stop.
6 Round off by going around the class and asking each person to say one name which the others echo back.

ONE-TO-ONE

1 Proceed as above.
2 Ask the student to put the names into two categories: 'Ones I can say easily' and 'Ones I have difficulty with'.
3 Work more on the difficult ones.

Circle intonation – names

1 CHILDREN'S SHOE SHOP
2 PETE'S SHIPPING AND REMOVALS
3 CAROL'S EARRINGS AND JEWELLERY
4 BARKER'S BODY SHOP
5 ARAMIS ATHLETIC EQUIPMENT
6 BIG BOY TAKE OUT RESTAURANT
7 RIO GRANDE RAILROAD
8 DOCTOR SPOCK'S OFFICE
9 JAMES, JOHNSON AND SPINNER LEGAL ADVISORS
10 BEAUTY AND FASHION BAR
11 FRESH FISH AND SHRIMP MARKET
12 THESPIAN THEATRE CIRCLE
13 PANDORA'S PIZZA PARLOR

3.2

LEVEL
Elementary+

MATERIALS
A list of English business names

TIME
15 to 20 minutes

FOCUS
Pronunciation, especially intonation

ACKNOWLEDGEMENT
The idea comes from Curran (1976).

3.3

LEVEL
Intermediate

MATERIALS
Photocopies of
Dialogues A and B

TIME
20 minutes

FOCUS
Speaking/
Listening,
Telephone
awareness,
Practice in using
stress and
intonation

PAIRED DIALOGUES

Students used to listening for words and grammar only will be surprised to see how changes in intonation and stress can change the meaning of the words in the simple dialogue used here.

Procedure

1 Explain what intonation is and tell your students that it is a vital part of spoken language, especially on the telephone since we are unable to get clues from people's faces about the real meaning behind words. Give an example using the expression *come here*, first in a demanding way as a mother to a child, then in a very suggestive way, as to a lover. This shows that the same words can definitely take on different meanings.
2 Divide the class into pairs.
3 Give each pair a copy of Dialogues A and B.
4 Pairs read through the dialogue, and fit the two halves together.
5 Pairs read each sentence out loud and decide if it is a statement, question, or exclamation.
6 Next, students read each sentence several times, each time stressing a different word. By now the sense of their dialogue will begin to take shape and students can decide who the characters are. Some possibilities are: a husband and wife, a boss and secretary, a young man and woman, two fussy old women, a businessperson and a client, etc.
7 Ask each pair to decide who will be A and who will be B. Pairs read the dialogues in role. Encourage students to change roles several times and experiment with their readings.

ONE-TO-ONE
As above.

ACKNOWLEDGEMENT
The dialogue is based on 'Silence', a short play by Harold Pinter.

WORKSHEET FOR ACTIVITY 3.3

Dialogue A

A Come out with me tonight

B

A Anywhere for a walk

B

A Why not

B

A Where

B

A What do you want to do

B

A Do you want to go anywhere else

B

A Where

B

Dialogue B

A

B Where

A

B I don't want to walk

A

B I want to go somewhere else

A

B I don't know

A

B I don't know

A

B Yes

A

B I don't know

© Longman Group Ltd. 1995 Photocopiable

3.4

LEVEL
Lower
Intermediate+

MATERIAL
None

TIME
20 minutes

FOCUS
Speaking,
Receiving and
transferring
messages,
Reported Speech

BACK-TO-BACK TELEPHONE MESSAGES

Students practise taking down messages for others in the group. To create the impression of being on the telephone, students sit back-to-back.

Procedure

1 Students form pairs sitting in chairs placed back-to-back.
2 Each student writes down a telephone message for a member of the class other than their partner. Messages should include:
   ● Name of person the message is for
   ● Name of person the message is from
   ● Reason for the call
   ● The caller's telephone number or a time when they will ring back.
3 Pairs take turns 'calling each other up' and taking down messages.
4 Students pass on messages to the third party. They do this orally by standing up and mingling or they write them down and pass them to the intended receiver. Example: *Message for Tom Harlow – John Davis called from Techniphon. He's having problems with his new installation. Call him back a.s.a.p. Tel. 379 42 90*

ONE-TO-ONE
You will need some other English-speaking friends, colleagues, or students who agree to help you. These people will:
● Call your student at a pre-arranged time and give them a message for you.
● Take down a message that you have previously given to your student.

3.5

LEVEL
Elementary+

MATERIALS
Photocopy of the
Telephone
Interview sheet
for each student

TIME
30 minutes

FOCUS
Dealing with
telephone anxiety

TELEPHONE AWARENESS INTERVIEW

Telephoning is one of the hardest things to do in a foreign language and students at all levels experience anxiety. We try to help students with telephone anxiety by breaking the problem down into steps they are familiar with and know they can handle. A good place for them to start is just expressing their anxieties and difficulties and becoming aware that this is a universal problem. That is exactly what we do in this first of a series of three frames for overcoming fear of phoning. The second frame focuses on outgoing calls and the third on incoming calls.

Procedure

1 Sit students back-to-back and stress they should not turn around during the activity. Give each a copy of the telephone interview. If you have an uneven number of students, make one group of three.

2 Tell them to ask and answer questions from the interview. They can ask as many questions as they wish, in any order. Make sure you monitor carefully and check to see that each student is both asking and answering.

3 After about ten minutes call a halt and ask the students what they thought of the activity. You will get comments about the difficulty of hearing well, about outside interferences and noises, not seeing the other student's face, etc. Ask which was more difficult, asking or answering questions.

4 Ask the students if they see similarities between the back-to-back interviews and being on the telephone. Bring the discussion around to what they find difficult about speaking on the phone. Ask a student to list these problems on the board.

5 Gradually bring the discussion around to possible solutions for each problem and write these ideas next to the problems on the board.

6 Now ask students to think about a typical telephone conversation. Isn't a phone call made up of three main phases? Try to elicit these.
- The first consists of greetings and identification. Elicit useful vocabulary and expressions. Write them on the board.
- The second phase is exchanging information. Somebody wants something from somebody else. Elicit further useful language, especially question and answer forms. Remind students of the use of *Wh*-questions.
- The final phase is signalling that the conversation should end and saying goodbye. This will probably be the phase in which the students have the least linguistic knowledge. You can help by giving them a few phrases such as *I really must let you get back to work. Thanks very much for your information. You've been very helpful and I appreciate it.* etc.

7 Make sure that each student has noted the particular expressions for each of the three phases. Ask students to compare their notes. Tell them to save them as they'll need them for the activities on outgoing and incoming calls (3.6, 3.7).

ONE-TO-ONE
As above, with the teacher playing a part.

WORKSHEET FOR ACTIVITY 3.5
Telephone interview

1 Can you spell your middle name?

2 Can you spell the name of your company?

3 What is your telephone number at home? At work?

4 What does your company do or make?

5 How many people work in your company?

6 Where is your company's headquarters?

7 How long have you worked in your present job?

8 What was your first job?

9 Have you got other people sharing your office? What are their names?

10 What and where is Wall Street?

11 What is the name of the President of the United States?

12 What do TWA and JAL stand for?

13 Can you name some English or American newspapers or magazines?

14 Do you travel for your job?

15 Tell me about something enjoyable you did on your last holiday.

OUTGOING CALLS STRATEGY

Students can help themselves a lot by simply realising that they can plan ahead for most of the telephone situations they encounter. In this second phase of breaking down telephone calls into familiar steps for students, we look at a strategy for preparing an outgoing call.

Procedure

1 Elicit the phases of a typical telephone call. If you have not done this before look at activity 3.5 for guidelines).

2 Ask your students how they can prepare ahead for an outgoing call. Write any ideas up on the board.

3 Ask each student to choose three typical situations where they have to make an outgoing call. For example, secretaries calling for hotel information, technicians calling for technical details, or employees checking on administrative information. Students describe these situations to each other and form pairs with another student who has similar kinds of outgoing calls.

4 Hand out copies of the Plan of Action for an Outgoing Call sheet (see page 54) and read them through with your students, encouraging comments.

5 Pairs work for ten or fifteen minutes preparing two typical telephone conversations.

6 Pairs role play their calls for the others.

7 Now ask students how this plan of action can help them in their everyday telephone business.

3.6

LEVEL
Elementary+

MATERIALS
Photocopy of Plan of Action for an Outgoing Call sheet for each student

TIME
30 minutes

FOCUS
Dealing with outgoing telephone calls

WORKSHEET FOR ACTIVITY 3.6
Plan of action for an outgoing call

Before you call:

1 Gather together all necessary information about the person you are calling:
- telephone number including extensions
- name and position of the person you are calling
- name and position of any other people you know in the company such as secretaries or people who can help you if things go wrong

2 Organise information to be used during the call; make a list or have the facts you will need at hand:
- letters with reference numbers
- files
- figures, graphs, calendars, or charts you may need to refer to
- names, addresses, and phone numbers of third parties

3 Try and foresee any questions the person you are calling might ask. Use this list of question words to help you:
- who?
- where?
- when?
- how (many, much, often, long)?
- why?

Can you answer the questions you expect to be asked?

On the phone:

1 Say your name and the name of your company. Give your reason for calling. You will usually ask for a person by name, or ask to speak to someone who can help you with your particular demand.

Example:

This is Jean Dupont calling from Innovac in France, may I speak to Bill Collins, please?

Hello, I'm Françoise Leport from Air France, could you tell me who is responsible for travel arrangements in your company?

2 Before making the call you gathered and organised facts to be used during the call, for example, files, reference numbers, etc. Use these facts now to help you ask for the information you need.

3 After you have got the information you wanted, you should signal that you wish to end the call. Use polite phrases which:

a thank the person for their help: 'Thank you very much, this information will complete my chart.'

b indicate that you are expecting action to happen as a result of this telephone call: 'That's great, I'll be expecting that cheque in the mail next week then. Thanks very much.'

INCOMING CALLS STRATEGY

In this third phase of breaking down telephone calls into familiar situations for students, we look at the strategy needed to prepare for incoming calls. Callers usually want the same kinds of information. By thinking ahead and organising that information, students can prepare for most of their incoming calls.

Procedure

1 Elicit the phases of a typical telephone call. If you have not done this before, look at activity 3.5 for guidelines.
2 Point out to the group that a person making an incoming call is usually someone looking for information, so the information exchange phase is very important here. Ask the students to think back over the last few weeks and remember all the different kinds of information they had to give out over the telephone. Write these on the board.
3 Ask each student to choose two typical situations where they receive incoming calls.
4 Describe these situations to the group. Form pairs of students having similar incoming call situations.
5 Hand out the copies of the Plan of Action for Incoming Calls (see page 56). Read the plan through with your students. Ask them for comments along the way.
6 Pairs work for ten or fifteen minutes and prepare two typical telephone conversations.
7 Pairs role play their calls for the others.

3.7

LEVEL
Elementary+

MATERIALS
Photocopy of Plan of Action for Incoming Calls sheet for each student

TIME
30 minutes

FOCUS
Dealing with incoming telephone calls

WORKSHEET FOR ACTIVITY 3.7
Plan of action for incoming calls

Before you receive a call:

1 Think about your working situation and the organisation of your company. What kinds of telephone inquiries do you receive? Make a list of the types of calls and the action you could take as a result.

Example:

QUESTIONS ABOUT	ACTION TO TAKE	WHO CAN HELP
invoices	payment	finance/Jean Dupont
spare parts	find reference	me
....	....	....
....	....	....
....	....	....
....	....	....

2 Now think in more detail about the calls you receive. List some of the questions you hear – not forgetting to use *who, what, when, how much, how many, how long, how often.*

1 ....?
2 ....?
3 ....?
4 ....?
5 ....?

On the phone:

1 Answer the telephone with a cheery greeting and present yourself or your company.
Example:
– Good morning, French Perfumes, Ltd.
– Good afternoon, Coca-Cola Spain.
– Hello, Ecole des Mines, Jean Dufour's office, Françoise speaking.
– Hello, finance department, Margaret Simpson.

2 The caller will then introduce her/himself and give the reason for calling. You must either put the caller through to another department or person or give the information yourself.
Examples:

CALLER	YOU
Hello, this is Bill Spikes.	
Is Jean Dupont in?	Yes, of course. One moment, please.
Good morning, Bob Jones.	
Is Françoise in?	No, I'm sorry. Can I help you?

Hello, Bob's motorbikes, could I speak to the person responsible for invoices please?	Yes, that would be Mr. Jones. Hold on please.
Hi, this is Sally Jackson. Would you happen to know last month's sales figures?	Sure. One minute and I'll just get them.
Hello, Jack. What time is the lunch today?	Twelve sharp. See you then

3 You are not the one needing information so it's not your role to signal that the call is over. However, if your caller doesn't seem to want to end the conversation, you can politely excuse yourself by saying you have another call or are wanted on another line.

© Longman Group Ltd. 1995 Photocopiable

TELEPHONE ROLE PLAYS

Students work in pairs to create a telephone conversation inspired by an authentic document. Invite the students to bring in their own documents, so that their work comes into the classroom. Otherwise you can provide documents.

Procedure

1 Ask students to form pairs.
2 Tell them to create a telephone dialogue using information from a document a student has brought in or to choose one of your documents.
3 Give them ten to fifteen minutes preparation time.
4 Using telephones or back-to-back chairs, pairs role play and record their conversation.
5 Pairs listen to their recordings, make any changes or improvements they want and re-record.
6 Each pair plays their final recording to the group.

ONE-TO-ONE
As above asking a friend, colleague or other English-speaking student to do the role play with your student.

NOTE
Toy walkie-talkie type telephones or used real ones can be used for the telephone link-up.

Here is an example of how one class decided to do a role play using the document in Fig. 9.

3.8

LEVEL
Intermediate+

MATERIALS
A telephone link-up, a selection of short business documents

TIME
30 minutes

FOCUS
Reading authentic documents, Listening and speaking, Telephoning

◼ *Stein Engineering Limited* ◼

FAX

To	Mr. Masson	**Your fax number**	0943 617348
From	Mr. V Steinhauser	**Our fax number**	0465 784367
Date	31 August	**Number of pages**	1
Subject	Yoghurt manufacturing machinery		

Dear Mr. Masson

This is to confirm that our engineer will arrive 4 September and stay for between one and two weeks in order to adjust the first yoghurt machine and supervise the production of the second.

Fig. 9

With this document, students decided that the fax was sent to confirm an earlier telephone conversation which they would role play. In their role played conversation Mr. Masson phoned Mr. Steinhauser to tell him that there were problems with two machines used in manufacturing yoghurt. Mr. Steinhauser asked some technical questions to see if they could solve the problems by giving instructions over the phone. When it became clear that this would not be possible, Mr. Steinhauser agreed to send an engineer to make the necessary repairs. They agreed upon an arrival date and the length of stay.

TELEPHONE TREASURE HUNT

This activity sends students on a real treasure hunt, seeking information from other people over the phone. Some would like to find out about other people's jobs or compare their own jobs to someone else's. Others simply appreciate having some practice speaking and listening on the phone.

Preparation

Ask some English-speaking friends or colleagues to be available at a given time to receive telephone calls from your students. Ask each volunteer what topics they would be ready to discuss on the phone. Make a list of these topics for the students to use in preparation for their phone calls.
Example:

Name	Topics
Luca Baggio, 60 24 39 48	His job in marketing, holidays in England, dogs, Chinese cooking.
Fiona Fields, 60 68 69 70	Her job as a receptionist, her education, horse-riding.
Joanna Billings, 43 24 17 72	Her job as a teacher, the American West, Canadian people, driving rules in America, vegetarian meals.

Procedure

1 Put your students in pairs.
2 Give each pair a list of people they can phone along with the telephone number and the topics about which each person is willing to speak.
3 Tell the students that they should make two phone calls per pair, but to the same person. Each call should be about four to seven minutes long. During this time they must ask the people on the list some questions about the topics they have agreed to speak about.
4 Each pair decides who to phone and the topic(s) they will ask questions about. Both students must speak on the phone. Different pairs can call the same people or different people as they wish and depending on how many willing English-speaking friends and colleagues you could find.
5 Students prepare questions. Allow about fifteen minutes. Each pair should have at least ten questions (or more) ready. This preparation time is vital and should not be omitted.
  ● Go from group to group, helping with basic sentence construction and reminding the students that, if they want to be understood, their sentences should be very simple and easy to understand, especially on the telephone.
  ● Pronunciation is also very important on the phone, so in each

3.9

LEVEL
Elementary+

MATERIALS
A telephone for one external call per student, some English-speaking people available to receive calls

TIME
60 minutes

FOCUS
Reported speech, Asking questions and gathering information, Practice in listening and speaking on the telephone, Writing up dialogues

pair ask students to mark the questions that they especially want to practise saying. Help with pronunciation and intonation work.

● Remember also to check each group's knowledge of basic telephone language (greetings/goodbyes, asking to speak to someone, cutting off the conversation, etc.). Give students help if they don't know these expressions.

6 As each pair finishes composing and practising their questions, they leave to make their phone calls. Remind them that *everyone* must speak on the phone. Meanwhile, the remaining pairs continue working on their questions and pronunciation.

7 When each pair finishes their phone calls, they write up the phone conversations either as a dialogue or in reported form, depending on the level of the group.

8 Students then read their phone conversation reports or role play their dialogues to the other pairs.

9 The group decides which pair got the most 'treasure' (quantity of information or most interesting facts). There will be different ideas as to how to judge or quantify the information. Let students discuss and make their own decisions here.

ONE-TO-ONE

1 Same as above.

2 Your student writes up the conversation as homework.

3 During the next session you and your student role play the dialogue or the student reads their reported speech dialogue out loud.

VARIATIONS

1 If there is only one person who can be called, have all of the groups prepare questions for the same people/person on the same topic(s). One by one, each person from each group in turn asks one or two of these questions to the person on the phone. Students then pool their information and each group together writes up a dialogue or report. Groups then compare reports or dialogues to see which one got the most (or the most interesting) information. The questions asked can also be compared at this time, to decide which ones were the best.

2 If there is a long list of people available and perhaps more than one telephone, have each group call each person but set a limit of two or three questions per call. Then, after comparing reports, students see which group got the most 'treasure' from their phone calls.

3 If phoning times are organised in advance, students can do telephone calls or the written reports (or both) outside of class time.

NOTE

The timing of this exercise is very important because people will be expecting to be called around a certain time. So you must plan ahead, and give students ample time for the preparation of their calls. Monitor time as they make their calls.

CHAPTER 4

Business communication in writing

An ability to communicate in writing is rapidly becoming essential with the ever increasing use of fax machines and electronic mail. However, when using traditional business communication exercises to teach writing skills, we have noticed a lack of motivation and interest even among students who need and ask for improvement in this area. We have found that adding an element of competition, a game, or a problem to solve can work magic. In this chapter there is a varied selection of activities which teach essential business writing skills in an active, enjoyable, and communicative way.

TRANSLATION GAME

This is a stimulating activity for students who need and enjoy translation. Here students serve as 'living dictionaries' for each other.

Procedure

1 Divide the group into pairs of students who have two common languages: usually their native language and English.
2 Set a writing task. This can be:
   ● a letter
   ● a product description
   ● a narrative, etc.
3 Student A does the task in English and student B does it in the other language. They work alone.
4 A and B exchange and translate each other's work into the other language. They are free to consult each other during this translation phase. You monitor their work and give any help or advice which is needed.
5 Gather up the translations and make any necessary corrections. If possible, type them up and give them back to students.

NOTE
In multi-level groups the activity works best by having the stronger students do their original writing in English and the weaker ones do the writing in their native language.

4.1

LEVEL
Intermediate+

TIME
45 minutes

FOCUS
Translating

REQUIREMENT
If your class is monolingual, you need to know their mother tongue well. If the class is multilingual, there should be at least two speakers of each mother tongue. You need to speak all of the languages represented.

ONE-TO-ONE
If your knowledge of your student's language is sufficient, you can do the above activity with your student.

ACKNOWLEDGEMENT
The idea for this activity comes from Mario Rinvolucri.

4.2

LEVEL
Intermediate

MATERIALS
Paper and pencil

TIME
30 minutes

FOCUS
Defining terms

DEFINITIONS

This exercise gets students really interested in writing. It can fit into various phases of a lesson. For example, it can precede work on a reading or listening activity, or provoke discussion around a theme or, at the end of a class, sum up what has been done.

Procedure

1 Select two terms you wish your students to define. For example *artificial intelligence* and *human intelligence*.
2 Ask your students to take out a piece of paper and a pen and form pairs facing each other.
3 One of the pair writes one of the terms at the top of their paper. The other writes the second term at the top of theirs.
4 Everyone writes their own definition for the term on their paper.
5 Pairs exchange papers and read each other's definitions. Everyone chooses a word from their partner's definition, underlines it, and then writes their own definition of that word.
6 Pairs again exchange papers, read definitions and repeat Step 5.
7 Continue this process at least five but not more than ten times.
8 Put papers up on the wall so that students can move around and read all the definitions.
9 To finish off you could set a writing task asking the students to use some of the defined words.

ONE-TO-ONE
You and your student write definitions back and forth to each other. Don't correct what your student writes as this would interfere with the spirit of equality in this activity. However, in your definitions you can include structures and vocabulary which the student can then use as models.

RATIONALE
Business people often need to clarify terms. This activity gives them practice at doing just that and at the same time lets them share vocabulary and new structures with each other.

THREE OBJECTS

Engineers and technicians work with descriptive language. This activity gives them the opportunity to practise describing objects. They decide which objects they wish to write about.

Procedure

1 Ask everyone to write down on a sheet of paper the names of three objects they use in their jobs. For example, objects could be a computer, a notebook, a telephone, a desk, a pen, a typewriter, an oscilloscope, a ruler, etc.
2 They exchange papers.
3 Everyone writes a short description of each of the three objects and then passes the paper back to the person it came from.
4 In small groups, students each name their objects and read out their descriptions. Then the group lists examples of possible documents where they could find such descriptions, for example: in reports, advertisements, catalogue listings, inventories, etc.
5 Tell the group that everyone is going to write a short text incorporating the three descriptions of the objects.
6 Offer your students the choice of completing the writing task in class or as homework.
7 Students read their paragraphs out loud to practise such microskills of oral presentation as accuracy in pronunciation, variation of tone and volume, and achieving good eye contact.
8 Collect the texts and type them up, making any necessary corrections but not changing or adding to the text content. Later, put these corrected versions on the wall for everyone to read and enjoy.

ONE-TO-ONE

1 You and your student do the above activity together.
2 Type up both paragraphs for easy reading.
3 Allow time at the next class for your student to practise reading the texts out loud. Work on stress by having your student mark words which should be stressed. In addition, give guidance about intonation.
4 You and the student read the two texts out loud to one another.

4.3

LEVEL
Intermediate

TIME
60 minutes

FOCUS
Describing objects, Writing, Listening, Speaking, Reading

4.4

LEVEL
Elementary+

MATERIALS
A box of
Cuisenaire rods,
some small brown
paper bags

TIME
45 minutes

FOCUS
Following
instructions,
Reading/Writing

THE INSTRUCTION MANUAL

This activity is for engineers, technicians, and computer operators who have to read technical instructions. It works well at all levels because the instructions students write should reflect their language level, e.g. elementary students are likely to use lots of imperatives, while higher level students may use constructions like *Once you have done . . ., do . . .* or *After installing . . ., place the. . . .*

Preparation

Decide how many pairs or small groups you will have. For each one prepare a paper bag with an equal number of Cuisenaire rods of the same colour and length. The number of rods each pair/group will get depends on their level; we suggest sixteen rods for intermediates. If you don't have Cuisenaire rods in your school, you can use Lego blocks, or various office supplies such as paperclips, rulers, erasers, pencils, etc.

Procedure

1 Divide your class into groups and give each group a bag of rods.
2 Tell students they have ten minutes to build a self-supporting structure using all the rods.
3 They then have fifteen minutes to write out clear, precise instructions on how to build the structure.
4 Each group puts the rods and the written instructions back into their bag.
5 Groups exchange bags, follow the instructions in their new bag and build the structure.
6 Each group displays their structure and explains any difficulties they had in following the instructions. They discuss ways of making muddled instructions clearer.

ONE-TO-ONE
As above. For once the student may have the advantage!

DEFINE MY TERMS
Procedure

1 Give out the document (or the list of vocabulary).
2 Students each choose three words or phrases they know and would like to work with.
3 On separate slips of paper everyone writes a definition for each technical term they have chosen.
4 Distribute the papers at random.
5 Taking turns, students read out the definitions. The rest of the class listen carefully and match the definitions to the items on the list or in the text.

VARIATION

If your students respond well to competition, divide your class into two teams. The opposing team has to guess the term being defined without looking at the document or vocabulary list.

4.5

LEVEL
Elementary

MATERIALS
A list of technical terms of interest to the group, or a document with a specialised vocabulary. Small slips of paper or cards

TIME
40 minutes

FOCUS
Building competence in technical· vocabulary

4.6

WORD ASSOCIATIONS – WORK

LEVEL
Upper
Intermediate

MATERIALS
None

TIME
60 minutes

FOCUS
Vocabulary
building, Writing

Students often say they can't write well because they don't have enough vocabulary. This activity builds vocabulary by getting students sharing words they already know in order to complete a writing task.

Procedure

STAGE ONE: BRAINSTORMING VOCABULARY

1 On the board write WORK in large letters.
2 Next write NOUNS.
3 The group brainstorms all the nouns they associate with the word work.
4 Do the same by writing VERBS and finally ADJECTIVES on the board.

STAGE TWO: WRITING

5 Students individually write a paragraph entitled WORK using the vocabulary from Stage One.

STAGE THREE: INTEGRATING

6 Students form groups of three.
7 They read their paragraphs to each other.
8 They then work together to re-write a new paragraph integrating elements from each student's original paragraph.
9 Paragraphs are read out loud or put on the walls for all to enjoy.

ONE-TO-ONE
Same as above with a dictionary or thesaurus for help.

ACKNOWLEDGEMENT
We learned this activity from Henri Sagot.

E-MAIL EASY ANSWER

Many professional people today have access to electronic mail. This is a very immediate and convenient system of communication but it's not always the best. Going over the e-mail Reminder Sheet helps students decide when e-mail is a better idea than a phone call or a fax. And a short, creative game at the end makes for a bit of writing practice.

Procedure

1 Give everyone a copy of the e-mail Reminder Sheet (see page 68).
2 In plenary read over and discuss the ideas on this sheet. Be sure to elicit real personal situations and get students to tell when and if each idea has been a part of their own experience. This time of sharing helps students to become more aware of the advantages and shortcomings of different communicative processes in the business world.
3 Write the following on the board and ask students to discuss it: *E-mail is really at its best when there is only one idea which requires an immediate answer.*
4 Form pairs and give each person a sheet of white paper.
5 Tell students to imagine and write a short e-mail type of proposal at the top of the sheet and fold it over. For example:
   – 'John, how about lunch today in the cafeteria?'
   – 'Research group one: meeting for new water cooling project projected for 2 p.m. on Tuesday 12th. OK for you?'
6 Students exchange papers, unfold, read and write an answer to the proposal. Before passing the paper back to their partner they write a proposal of their own which their partner will respond to. This exchange can continue as long as students continue to ask and answer questions.
7 Put the exchanges up on the wall. Pairs circulate and read them.

NOTE
Of course, if you have access to a real e-mail system, this whole exercise can be done on the system.

VARIATION
Another way of using the e-mail Reminder Sheet is to play a quick memory game. Read the e-mail Reminder Sheet out loud together in class, then ask students to turn it over and see who can remember the most of the thirteen different ideas.

ONE-TO-ONE
Same as above, though the memory game variation works especially well here.

4.7

LEVEL
Intermediate

MATERIALS
A photocopy of the e-mail Reminder Sheet for each student (example below)

TIME
30 minutes

FOCUS
Awareness of e-mail, Writing

WORKSHEET FOR ACTIVITY 4.7

E-mail reminder sheet

1 To use e-mail you have to be able to type.

2 In lots of companies people can use e-mail at home as well as at work so e-mail encourages prompt, spontaneous communication. Time zones no longer exist – a message from the other side of the world can be dealt with immediately.

3 For secretaries an e-mail is a very quick and sure way of leaving a message.

4 E-mail gives lots of identifying information, like who sent the message, at what time, when it arrived, and who else has received it.

5 The big question is, 'Should I send my message e-mail or pick up my phone?' If there is only one piece of information to be acted upon, e-mail is OK. If a discussion is necessary, then e-mail will become long and complicated. A phone call would be better.

6 If you have two or three subjects to cover, you must send one e-mail per subject. If a person can't answer all the problems presented in a mail, they will probably put it off or not answer at all.

7 E-mail has your name on it so it can be used as proof of what you have said. This is not the case with a phone call.

8 Achieving the right level of formality can be a problem. Since there is no intonation or tone of voice as on the phone, words count. Decide how formal you want to be. In general, e-mail is less formal than a letter, so it tends to be used with people you know rather well. The usual tone is relaxed and friendly.

9 But be careful, e-mail should be 'boring'. Use straight delivery and say exactly what you want to say. No jokes or innuendos allowed here; they could come across differently to the way you intend as there's no vocal tone or facial expressions to help.

10 When someone sends e-mail they probably won't keep a copy, so you must remember to add something to your message to make it clear which e-mail is being answered. Sometimes you may answer a few days later and the sender might have forgotten all about their mail, so this reference becomes even more important than in the case of a paper letter or fax.

11 Since there is not necessarily a written record of the e-mail, you might like an acknowledgement of reception. You have to remember to ask for this in your message. (For example you can say, 'Please acknowledge this mail.')

12 Think very carefully about the subject heading that you announce in your e-mail identification. Some people receive lots of mail so they look directly at the subject and if you haven't been specific enough about this they might skip over your mail altogether.

13 Again, e-mail users often receive lots of mail, so if you want to broadcast something to lots of people (as when selling something) you should use the electronic bulletin board included in most electronic hook-ups, and not cause e-mail overloads to busy managers, engineers, or secretaries.

HOW TO GROW A FAX

Because of the fax, many people today in their work have to be able to understand and write simple messages in English. This activity gives students the ABC of where to start – by asking the right questions.

Preparation

Ask students to each bring in a fax. Have a few in reserve yourself in case someone forgets.

Procedure

STAGE ONE – READING AND UNDERSTANDING
1 Ask students to get out their faxes.
2 Put students in pairs and give everyone a copy of the Fax Questionnaire (see page 70).
3 Using their faxes and the questionnaire, ask each pair to answer the questions about 'fax ID' (the identifying information found in their faxes) and compare their answers. (They will realise that there is a standard format for fax ID.)
4 Now ask each pair to look at the main body of information being transmitted in their faxes and to answer the questions under 'fax information' on the questionnaire. (They will realise that the information is specific to the needs of their company.)
5 Ask pairs to discuss the differences and similarities for each document.
6 Ask pairs to see if there are any expressions, verbs, functions, etc. that recur throughout the faxes. Go through the meanings and uses of these and elicit others the students might know or have questions about.

STAGE TWO – WRITING YOUR OWN FAX
1 At the bottom of the Fax Questionnaire there are fax questions for a sender. Point this section out to your students and in plenary go over the questions with them.
2 Ask students to imagine a work situation where they would have to send a fax. In pairs have them describe these situations to each other.
3 Everyone writes their faxes. Each pair will write two different faxes.
4 Pairs exchange faxes and read them over, checking that all necessary information is there.

ONE-TO-ONE
Proceed as above.

4.8

LEVEL
Intermediate

MATERIALS
Faxes which students have brought in, A photocopy of the Fax Questionnaire for each student

TIME
45 minutes

FOCUS
Reading, deciphering, and writing a fax

WORKSHEET FOR ACTIVITY 4.8

Fax questionnaire

FAX ID

1 What is the date on the document?
2 What is the reference number? What does this refer to?
3 Who is the text from? What is their address, phone/fax number?
4 Who is the fax to? What is their address, phone/fax number?
5 Is the text intended for a special person (attention:)?
6 Are copies being sent to someone else?
7 What is the subject?

FAX INFORMATION

1 What is the reason this fax is being sent?
    – What reference is presented? (number, phone call, letter, fax, etc.)
    – What problem is presented?
2 What information or facts are being given?
    – numbers/quantities
    – names of people/places
    – times/dates
    – materials/articles/parts
    – means of transport

FAX QUESTIONS FOR A SENDER

1 What do you want the fax receiver to do?
2 Are there references or contact details for the receiver if they need further information?
3 Have you thanked them for their help/support/understanding/business/order/ etc.?
4 What do you say at the end of a fax?

ELECTRONIC TOURISM

Computers and modems can overcome geographical and social distances to bring people together who might never meet. Take your students on an electronic trip where they use this technology to exchange and share feelings, beliefs and ideas which they would perhaps hesitate to express face-to-face.

Preparation

Set up an exchange between two classes living and working in different companies, areas or countries. You can organise this through schools and institutions having a computer link-up or through multinational companies with an e-mail system.

Procedure

1 Students prepare questionnaires to send students in the other class. You give them no (or very little) information about the other class. Starting with short personal introductions, followed by personal queries, they move on to ask questions about values, ideas, personal opinions and so on.
2 Students take turns typing up these questions on the computer and classmates correct each other as they go along. Timing can be flexible here, as the computer will store the questions until your students are ready to send them.
3 The two classes send questions to each other.
4 Students read the questions they have received and see if they can draw conclusions about the other class.
5 They discuss each question, decide on answers and send them back.
6 Each class reads and discusses the answers to their questions.
7 Classes can send back and ask for more clarification or information.

ONE-TO-ONE

Computer networks let people express themselves without the usual clues of body, voice, clothing or even name. This provides a chance to play detective.

1 Set up a computer link between your student and someone else in a different country.
2 Each person writes a report on any current event or an economic or social situation in their country. They write this report impersonally, screening out all personal details such as age and background.
3 From the reports, each person analyses the content and tries to determine the sex, age, job, background, etc. of the other. Then they try to form a visual image of each other. They write these ideas down.

4.9

LEVEL
Intermediate+

TIME
4 hours over a short period of time (depending on the frequency of the class)

FOCUS
Reading/Writing

REQUIREMENT
A computer or telecommunication link-up between schools, companies or company branches

4 Students exchange their assessments and check them out to see to
   what extent they are accurate or inaccurate.

NOTE

In our experience about 50 per cent of the assessments are incorrect
because they are based on stereotyping. For example, one woman
misjudged the sex, believing a man was a woman because she felt his
report was illogical and, for her, women were in general illogical.

ACKNOWLEDGEMENT

Our thanks to Karen Blair in Geneva who has done research on uses
of computer technology in the foreign language classroom.

CHAPTER 5

Using authentic business documents

For many business and technical people, their only contact with English is through reading professional documents such as brochures, technical instructions and notices, reports, company newspapers, or balance sheets. This chapter contains activity frames describing how such documents can be made into interesting activities which you can apply to your students' documents. All of these documents are easily accessible and students are always delighted to see an activity created from something that is so directly applicable to their work.

SIMPLE ONE DOCUMENT WARM-UP

This activity is a good way to warm students up for work on a document or text connected to their work.

Procedure

1 Split the class into small groups. Give each group the same short authentic document.
2 Tell each group to write down ten questions that they can answer from information found on this document. With a group going to Oxford for a seminar, we presented them with two tour bus tickets of this beautiful university city. There was some information about the city and its history presented on the back of the ticket, so it was easy to ask questions about the tickets. But one group showed its originality by asking what colour and shape the ticket was, who could use it (adults or children), and how much it had cost.
3 Each group asks their questions in turn to the other team who finds the answers on the document as quickly as possible.

NOTE
We have found that students are delighted to handle a real English document and see that they can process the information it contains.

ONE-TO-ONE
As above.

5.1

LEVEL
Elementary+

MATERIALS
Enough identical short authentic documents (ticket, brochure, advert, letter, etc.) for each group to have one

TIME
30 minutes

FOCUS
Extracting information, Asking and answering questions

5.2

LEVEL
Elementary+

MATERIALS
A board for you to
write on and
paper for
students

TIME
20 minutes

FOCUS
Preposition
practice on a two-
dimensional plane

UPPER LEFT-HAND CORNER

This activity is one way of introducing prepositions and having a fun
practice session with them.

Procedure

1 In each corner of the board draw various figures (star, heart, circle,
square, cross, numbers, smiling face, etc.) and ask students to tell
you where they are. Introduce the terms *upper/lower, top/bottom,
left-hand/right-hand side*. You want answers like *The heart is in the
upper left-hand corner.*

2 Next draw figures in the centre of the whole layout and more figures
in the middle of each quarter (top left, bottom left, top right, and
bottom right). Ask students where the figures are. Elicit language
like *in the middle of the board* or *in the middle of the left-hand quarter*.
If you have elementary students, you will probably want to stop
here and follow on from Step 6 to have students practise the language they have just learnt.

3 For intermediate+ students, draw figures on the sides about a
quarter of the way down and on the top and bottom a third of the
way over (from the left or from the right). Ask students to describe
these positions. Here the language gets more complicated and you
want answers such as *The star is on the left-hand side, a quarter of
the way down from the top.* or *The heart is a third of the way over from
the left, on the top.*

An example of figures for upper left-hand corner is in Fig. 10.

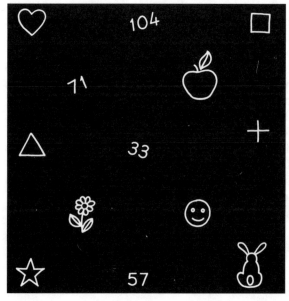

Fig. 10

4 Point out to your students that they are focusing on three important notions when locating items on a page:
- the distance in terms of proportion (one quarter, one third)
rather than in centimetres
- the direction (over, up, down)
- the starting point (from the left/right-hand side, the top, bottom)
Through questions, elicit the fact that a third of the way over from
the left is also two-thirds of the way over from the right. And that a
quarter of the way up is also three-quarters of the way down.

5 Finally, draw figures in places that require both horizontal and vertical description and get your students to say where these figures
are. For example *The star is one quarter of the way up from the bottom
and one quarter of the way over from the left-hand side.*

6 Ask each student to take an empty sheet of paper, fold it into quar-
ters, and write their first and last name somewhere on the paper.

7 Keeping their sheets covered, the students mingle and use the language they have just learnt to tell each other where they have
written their names. When told where a name is, students copy it
onto their sheet in that location. They continue until everyone has
all the names written on their papers.

8 Lay all the papers out on the table and compare – they should be
identical!

RATIONALE
Technical and business students often have to describe the position
of things on papers, drawings, spreadsheets, etc. either over the telephone or during presentations. This 'position' language which is so
necessary to their work is often a mystery to students.

NOTE
One thing to be aware of before starting this exercise, is that this language is good for only two-dimensional descriptions. Language
changes if you start describing rooms and places in space. You could
make this the focus of another exercise.

ONE-TO-ONE
As above.

ONE-TO-ONE EXTENSION (after Step 5)
1 Ask your student to write the names of people in their company in
different positions on a sheet of paper.
2 The student tells you each name and describes its position.
3 You write down the name in its position.
4 Compare your names and positions with your student's.

ONE-TO-ONE VARIATION
Do the above on the telephone.

5.3

LEVEL
Intermediate+

MATERIALS
Two company
brochures

TIME
45 minutes

FOCUS
Reading and
gathering
information,
Asking and
answering
questions

BROCHURES, BROCHURES

Any documents of interest to the group work well here. As the activity demands little or no preparation on your part, it is good for use when students have a technical speciality you don't feel particularly confident in.

Preparation

You need two company brochures. Ask students to bring them in or provide them yourself.

Procedure

1 Divide the group in half. Give each half a different brochure.
2 Students work together to read and understand their brochure. They then decide upon three separate words that sum up the content of their brochure.
3 Form pairs of students, one from each group.
4 Pairs exchange words. They ask 'yes and no' questions around the three words until they find out the content of each other's brochure.

ONE-TO-ONE
As above.

ACKNOWLEDGEMENT
Paul Davis shared this idea with us which he uses with short stories. He's not sure where the idea came from.

5.4

LEVEL
Intermediate+

MATERIALS
A range of
authentic
documents, Slips
of paper (see
Preparation)

TIME
45 minutes

FOCUS
Reading/writing
skills

FIRST SENTENCE

This game-like activity to develop reading skills brings down many of the barriers to reading technical documents.

Preparation

Find a selection of documents of interest to your group or ask students to bring some to class. Prepare enough slips of paper for each student to have at least as many slips as there are students in the class.

Procedure

1 Each person chooses a document at random.
2 Taking turns, students cover the first sentence with a slip of paper and then hold up their documents to the group. The object is for everyone to get an overall view of the document.

- length?
- title?
- are there any pictures, graphs, tables?
- mathematical formulae or calculations?

3 Each student chooses a short, representative paragraph from their document (but not the first paragraph).

4 One student reads their paragraph out loud to the group, being careful to read loudly and clearly so that everyone can hear and understand. This is so everyone can form a general idea as to what the document is about.

5 Now comes the fun part. After listening to the paragraph, ask students to write out on a slip of paper what the first sentence of that document might be. Meanwhile, the reader of the document writes the *real* first sentence on a slip of paper.

6 Mix all the slips together and give them to the reader.

7 The reader reads all the sentences out loud and each person in the group says which one they think is the real first sentence of the document.

8 Give one point to the reader for each person who guesses the real first sentence.

9 Ask students to vote on which made-up first sentence was the best. Give one point to the student who wrote that sentence.

10 Repeat Steps 4–9 until everyone has presented their document. Don't forget to count points!

ONE-TO-ONE

1 Before the lesson, select some documents and write the first sentence of each on a slip of paper. Ask your student to do the same.

2 In class, put all the slips on the table and both of you quickly read them through silently.

3 Ask your student to select a short representative paragraph from one of their documents (but not the first paragraph) and read it out to you. They must make sure you can't see the first sentence of the document!

4 Then you try to match one of the opening sentences on the table to that document. Give yourself one point if you are correct.

5 Repeat Steps 3 and 4, but this time you read a paragraph from one of your documents and your student tries to identify the opening sentence of the document.

6 Continue taking turns until you have dealt with all the documents.

ACKNOWLEDGEMENT
Thanks to Paul Davis for passing on this technique to us in Lancaster, June 1991.

5.5

LEVEL
Intermediate+

MATERIALS
Paper squares or index cards (41 or 42, see Preparation)

TIME
20 minutes

FOCUS
Awareness of the different styles of language used in business English

YOU'RE FIRED!

Business students come into contact with a lot of jargon. This exercise simplifies what seems complicated by breaking the meaning down into its simplest form.

Preparation

1 Before class, write each word of the following three sentences on separate paper squares or index cards. (You will have a total of 41 or 42 squares or cards, depending on whether you put *you're* on one card or two.)

We regret to inform you that, in order to streamline our liabilities and maximise our resources, it is incumbent on us to remove your current means of livelihood.
Due to restructuring, we shall be forced to terminate your employment.
You're fired!

2 Prepare one set for every five or six students.

Procedure

1 Give out a set of cards or paper squares to each group of students. Tell students that there are three sentences on the cards for them to sort out. Give enough time for them to sort out the sentences. Usually, students progress slowly until they have worked out the context.
2 Groups compare their sentences and decide on the correct reconstruction of each.
3 For each sentence ask if the language is appropriate in the following situations. Why/why not?
   – a written letter
   – someone making an announcement before a group
   – in a departmental meeting
   – face-to-face after a serious problem.
4 Continue discussion about levels of language, their differences, their importance, who uses them and in what kinds of situations. Students may want guidelines about linguistic characteristics of the 'complex' formulations. Here are a few ways to make language sound more formal:
   ● be less personal: use fewer pronouns, the passive voice reduces the need for pronouns. The passive voice is used often in business because it conceals who is responsible for an act. (e.g. 'It has been decided that there will be no pay rises this year.') The passive voice is often used in reports and technical papers because what's really important is not *who* but *what*. (e.g. 'The experiments were carried out in an atmosphere of 5% nitrogen.')
   ● use more 'nominalised' verbs (e.g. 'maximisation of resources . . .' instead of 'to maximise resources . . .').

- use more Latin or Greek derived vocabulary (e.g. 'my definitive response' instead of 'my last answer')
- use more 'compound' conjunctions and time expressions: (i.e. *moreover, hereafter, therefore*, etc.)

EXTENSION

Working in small groups, students choose one of the sentences and role play a situation where it would be appropriate.

VARIATION

More advanced students enjoy writing their own sentences. They can start with the most complex and move downwards, or vice versa. Other messages which could be put in different versions are:

'I want a raise.'

'There will be a takeover/merger.'

'The air controllers are going on strike again.'

5.6

LEVEL
Intermediate

MATERIALS
Photocopies of
Crazy Instructions
Texts

TIME
30 minutes

FOCUS
Giving and
understanding
instructions

CRAZY INSTRUCTIONS GAME

Giving and understanding instructions clearly is a very important skill to business and technical people. This amusing activity gives students practice, no matter what their job speciality is.

Procedure

1 Cut the crazy instructions out and give a different set of instructions to each student (see page 81). Put students into groups of six so that each student in a group has a different set of instructions. They should sit in two rows of three opposite each other. Everyone must read and memorise their instructions.

2 Turning to their partner – the person opposite them – students then tell each other their instructions, but only once. They should not take notes and so must listen very carefully.

3 Students change partners. To do this, the student sitting at the end of *one* of the rows of three in each group gets up and moves to the other end of their row and everyone in that row moves down one. When they have changed partners, this time students tell each other the instructions they have just heard, and not their original ones.

4 Students change partners again. The same rows of students as in Step 3 move down one place. They then repeat the last set of instructions that they heard. This makes three exchanges.

5 Students make a fourth change of partners and a final exchange of instructions.

6 Ask each student to repeat the last set of instructions that they heard to the rest of their group. Students listen carefully and try to recognise which instructions were their original ones.

7 When someone recognises their instructions, they say what has been changed or deformed with the original instructions. This is always very interesting, surprising, and a lot of fun.

8 As a group, discuss what kinds of things seemed to be deformed the most. Did the changes have to do with reality or fantasy? Did logical ideas or silly ones seem to be passed on more clearly? What can this teach us about giving instructions? What can this teach us about the way we listen and the way we present ideas?

WORKSHEET FOR ACTIVITY 5.6

Crazy instructions texts

FEMBURGER SALAD

Buy a jar of pickled Femburgers, some lettuce, a small quantity of olive oil and a large turnip. Cut the turnip into big bits and feed it to a pig. Put the lettuce on a plate, pile the Femburgers on top of the lettuce, pour the olive oil over the top, and eat your salad with a very sharp pin.

WHAT TO DO WHEN YOU GET TO A DANGEROUS FAST-FLOWING RIVER

Test the speed of flow with your little finger. Take four wooden logs and make a square. Take ten more logs and balance them on your head! Think hard. Walk away and eat some Rambawungus. Sit down and brew a cup of tea. Walk away rapidly.

TO MAKE A LARGE PILE OF EXCITING THINGS

Take a large number of exciting things. Put the biggest object at the bottom. Then take the next biggest object and put it on top, and so on. If your pile gets very large, use a ladder to get to the top. Remember to invite your neighbour to come and see it. Or if you don't want to invite them, don't.

RAMBAWUNGUS DELIGHT

Take one medium-ripe Rambawungus. Chop it up finely and leave it to soak in red wine for two months. After two weeks remove the Rambawungus and mash it to a thin pulp. Season to taste with salt, pepper, garlic and honey. Whip up half a tablespoon of cream and fold it into the mixture. Place it in a lovely crystal bowl and throw it all out of the window.

TO BUILD A SMALL HOUSE IN A STRANGE COUNTRY

Before you leave, be sure to pack a small house in your rucksack. When you want to build a new house, take the old one out and photocopy it carefully. Use the same materials as the model. If you can't find any, give up and go home! You're obviously not meant to be a traveller.

TO MAKE A CAGE FOR A LARGE ANIMAL

Take a baby large animal. Measure it carefully and add one hundred and eighty metres each way in case it grows. Arrange some tin cans in a circle. Lean several longish bits of wood against them. Then add a few old washing machines over the top. Decorate tastefully with bits of carrot and plastic carrier bags.

5.7

LEVEL
Elementary+

MATERIALS
An organigram or
organisation
chart, A box of
Cuisenaire rods
(optional)

TIME
30 minutes

FOCUS
Asking questions,
Describing
function and
relationships

ORGANIGRAM

Organigrams or company organisation charts can be easily obtained;
ask a student to bring one in. This activity can be done with students
of the same or different companies. We use this activity fairly early on
in all our courses because it is good for opening up shy or non-com-
municative students who very often don't see the point of speaking
English to each other.

Preparation

Prepare a basis for an information gap activity by blanking out names
and functions on one organisation chart. The activity can then be
done in a variety of ways:

● For whole group work, blank out different names and functions on
  each copy of the chart. Students mingle asking questions until
  they complete their charts.
● For groups of three, divide photocopies of the organigrams into
  three sets. In the first set blank out all the names, in the second
  blank out all the functions, and in the third set blank out everything so that only the boxes remain. Students work in groups of
  three to complete their organigrams.
● For pairwork, make two sets by blanking out the names in the first
  group and the functions in the second. Pairs share their information.

Procedure

1 Show students what an organigram is by illustrating one using the
  Cuisenaire rods. If you don't have any Cuisenaire rods, you can use
  coloured pencils. Students too may enjoy using the rods to illus-
  trate a group they belong to, for example, their family, religious
  organisation, social club or company.
  Example:

long orange rod

Board of Directors
Mr. Lewis, Mr. James, Mr. Smiley

yellow rod

Company President
Mr. Smiley

light green rod	light green rod	light green rod
Marketing Director	Sales Director	Head of Production
Ms. Elliott	Mr. St. Vrain	Mr. Stanley

2 Give out the previously prepared organigrams.

3 Students exchange the information on their charts by asking each other questions. To do this students need to be able to:

- use prepositions: *above, below, beside/next to, on the right/left of*
- spell names and ask how to spell someone's name.
- understand and describe job functions.
- ask questions to gather, clarify and confirm information.

VARIATION

With small groups of two to four students the information exchange can be done over the telephone to practise basic telephone skills.

ONE-TO-ONE

1 Ask your student to bring an organigram of their company.

2 Make a blown up photocopy of the organigram.

3 Cut it up and place the pieces in an envelope.

4 Give the student ten minutes to sort out the organigram and fit the pieces together while explaining it to you.

5 The student then prepares a description of their company based on the organigram. They can write it, present it live, or pre-record it and play it in class.

5.8

LEVEL
Elementary+

MATERIALS
Each student will
need to bring in a
visual aid or
object associated
with their job,
profession, or
company

TIME
30 minutes

FOCUS
Listening and
speaking,
Asking/answering
questions,
Describing

VISUAL INTERROGATION

This is a stimulating activity for groups of students who work in different companies or in large ones where different services have little or no contact with each other. Here, they have the chance to find out about each other.

Preparation

1 For the next class ask students to bring in a visual aid or a real object which they use in their job. For example:
- an illustration or logo
- a picture from the company brochure or an advertisement
- a diagram or illustration from a technical manual
- an object like a pocket calculator or pencil holder

It is important that students choose their own visual aid or object as this investment by the students adds value to the activity.

2 Ask them to write down twelve words they associate with their visual aid/object.

Procedure

1 In class, ask students to form pairs. They are not to show their visual aid/object but keep it out of sight. Ask them each to exchange their list of twelve words.
2 Using these lists, pairs question each other to find out as much as possible about their partner's visual aid/object in order to form a mental image of it.
3 After the questioning phase, pairs draw each other's visual aid/object.
4 They compare their drawings with the thing itself.

NOTE
Often teachers shy away from asking business people and technicians to draw. However, engineers, technicians, and draftspeople are very comfortable with this mode of communication.

VARIATION
Students exchange word lists either before or after questioning, or during questioning if their partner seems to need prompting.

ONE-TO-ONE
As above.

ONE-TO-ONE RATIONALE
This activity encourages empathetic communication between you and your student. It is generally an eye-opener for you as you both find out a lot about each other's job.

WRITING ON THE WALL

This is a good way to work with short texts and documents. It works well when students' energy levels are low and they need an activity which provides movement and interaction.

Preparation

1 Choose twelve short texts and place them on the walls around the room taking care to spread them out. For a lower intermediate class, we choose texts from a British newspaper: exchange rates bulletins, cinema listings, radio programmes, sports features, TV programme listings, an advert for furniture, an announcement for a mass meeting, holiday adverts, and a list of guided visits.
2 Make up a questionnaire based on information found in the posted texts. You need around 15 questions of the *Who/What/When/How* type. For example: *Where was the temperature the hottest today? What will be on Radio Four at 6 p.m.?*

Procedure

1 Divide the class into two teams and give each a copy of the questionnaire.
2 Give the teams time to read and understand the questions.
3 Tell the groups that this is a contest to see which group can complete their questionnaire with the right answers first.
4 After each group has finished filling in their questionnaire, bring the groups back together to compare answers.

NOTE

If competition works well in the culture where you are teaching, this stimulating game can be a real energy builder. If the culture is not competitive, this activity can still encourage students to organise cooperative group work.

ONE-TO-ONE

1 Give about twenty minutes for the student to fill in the questionnaire before reporting their information back to you.
Or
2 You and your student compete and see who can find the information the fastest. (The student gets a handicap or a head start!)

VARIATION

After the original game, the student makes up a questionnaire of this type for you, using a company document.

5.9

LEVEL
Intermediate

MATERIALS
Twelve short texts taken from a newspaper, or professional documents such as brochures, letters, faxes, diagrams, etc.

TIME
30 minutes

FOCUS
Information gathering, Speed reading for facts

5.10

LEVEL
Intermediate

MATERIALS
Copies of several letters to the editor about the same topic from any periodical or current events magazine

TIME
60 minutes

FOCUS
Reading/Speaking, Giving opinions, Recognising different points of view

LETTERS TO THE EDITOR

Magazines with readers' comments about previous articles provide a rich source of varied classroom material. The letters give students a window onto how native speakers express agreement or disagreement and give their point of view on a topic. Additionally, they often gain insight into differences in value systems and other elements of culture.

Preparation

1 Before class find a series of letters to the editor about a topic of interest to the group.
2 Cut them out, arrange and glue them onto one piece of A4 paper.
3 Give each a number and write this number below each letter.
4 Make photocopies.

Procedure

1 Give out the copies of the letters. If you want students to work together, give one copy to every third or fourth student; groups will form naturally around each copy.
2 Ask students to read through the letters rather quickly and to underline words or phrases which they think express opinions or points of view.
3 Ask them to call out the examples they find. You write these up on the board. Explain and discuss wherever necessary.
4 Next, ask everyone to re-read the letters in order to decide if the author of the letter expressed an opinion for or against the topic. They fill in a grid like the one in Fig. 11, using the numbers you have written on the letters to the editor. Rank opinions farthest left as 'for' and opinions farthest right as 'against'.
5 Ask students to re-read the letters again. This time they look for clues as to whether or not the author of the letter approved or disapproved of the magazine's point of view expressed during their coverage of the topic. Once more students rank these on a grid, like the one in Fig. 12.

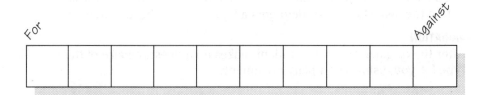

Fig. 11

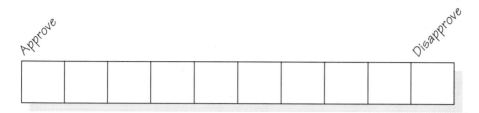

Fig. 12

6 Either individually or in groups, ask students to write their own letters to the editor about the topic.

RATIONALE

Ranking letters of this type provokes discussion during which students express their own opinions and points of view while reading about the opinions and points of view of other people.

GUTTING THE NEWSPAPER

Students want to read English language newspapers but often find them too difficult and become discouraged. Here students come into contact with a newspaper and its content without having to wade through a long, mostly incomprehensible article.

Procedure

1 Hand out a photocopy of the contents list (minus the page numbers) from an English language newspaper to every four or five students. These students work together in a group.
2 Briefly discuss the purpose of the list and clarify the meanings of any of the items which are unknown.
3 Ask students to predict what type of information they will find under each item.
4 Give out a newspaper, a pair of scissors and glue to each group.
5 Students 'gut' the newspaper and find a short example of each item on the list. They glue the list in the middle of a sheet of paper and arrange their examples around it.
6 Bring the groups back together. Everyone shares one or two examples they have found with the others.

VARIATIONS

1 With different groups (of lower levels) use the sheets that you have already created in Step 5 above as matching exercises. Hand them out and ask students to draw lines from the articles to the items in the contents list and explain their choices.
2 With lower level groups, keep page numbers on the contents lists.

5.11

LEVEL
Lower
intermediate+

MATERIALS
An English
language
newspaper
contents list,
scissors and glue

TIME
20–30 minutes

FOCUS
Reading skills

ONE-TO-ONE

1 Give the student the photocopy of the contents list.
2 Ask them to buy a copy of any English newspaper after class.
3 For homework, the student looks through the paper and finds an example of each item in the contents list you have given them.

5.12

LEVEL
Intermediate+

MATERIALS
Multiple copies of two texts sharing a common subject but written from different points of view

TIME
45 minutes

FOCUS
Asking and answering questions, Comparing and contrasting

PARALLEL TEXTS
Preparation

Find two texts which are about the same subject from two different sources. These sources can be different newspapers, magazines, or brochures for the same product or service, for example insurance company brochures. News magazines such as *Time* and *Newsweek* often cover the same story with variations on facts. Students can test their command of the language against a source originally designed for native speakers.

Procedure

1 Divide the class into two halves.
2 Give each half one of the two texts to read.
3 Ask groups to make up some general comprehension questions about their text. Each student needs a copy of these questions and a copy of their text.
4 Form pairs taking one student from each group.
5 Students take turns asking their questions to each other. Since their partner's answers will be based on the text the *other* group has read, each student finds out about the other text, sometimes with surprising results.
6 Each pair makes a list of similarities and differences in the two texts, again *without reading* their partner's text.

ONE-TO-ONE
As above.

ONE-TO-ONE VARIATION
Use cross-lingual parallel texts, one in English, one in the student's native language (if you know this language well enough). The student works on the English text and you on the other one. This process opens the student's eyes (and perhaps yours!) to all kinds of useful equivalent expressions between the two languages.

THE STUDENT'S DOCUMENT

This activity is especially useful when a student wants to work on one of their own documents. Very often the others in the class may lack interest in this. But THE STUDENT'S DOCUMENT gets everyone involved through predicting, note-taking, listening, and discussion.

Preparation

 Ask a student to choose a document of personal interest and prepare a five-to-ten minute oral presentation for the next class.

Procedure

1 This student reads only the title to the rest of the group.
2 Form pairs or groups and ask them to jot down everything they think might come up in a document with that title: facts, opinions, organisational details, statistics, figures, graphs, charts, or other visuals. Give a time limit of ten minutes.
3 Meanwhile, the student who is going to give the talk about the document rehearses or goes over their presentation with you.
4 The student gives their talk and everyone takes notes.
5 After the talk, students compare their predictions with the actual facts and ideas presented and draw up a list of differences.
6 The student who presented the talk goes around to each group and deals with any points that remain unclear or that were not properly understood.
7 Bring the group back together. The speaker gives everyone a copy of the document.
8 Students compare what was presented in the presentation to what was actually written in the document.

VARIATION

Ask each student about to come on a residential course to bring a document representative of their work or their home country.

ONE-TO-ONE

1 You do the work described in Step 2.
2 The student presents their talk to you.
3 After the talk, you and your student compare your predictions with the content of the talk.
4 If some aspects of the document were presented but not others, draw the student out about their criteria for selecting and rejecting what to present.

5.13

LEVEL
Intermediate+

MATERIALS
A document which one of the students wants to work on. This may be a brochure, a set of instructions, a newspaper article, a text, a company advertisement, or even a complex technical document

TIME
45 minutes

FOCUS
Giving a talk, Listening and note-taking

5.14

LEVEL
Elementary+

MATERIALS
A short text, index
cards

TIME
30 minutes

FOCUS
Listening and
writing/note-
taking, Organising
a text

JIGSAW PUZZLE NOTE-TAKING

This activity is good for working on authentic texts as it encourages students to reach for global meaning instead of trying to understand each word separately.

Preparation

1 Before class choose a short text of interest to the group. The first time you do this choose a text which has a clear chronological order emphasised by lots of link words such as 'first', 'then' and 'finally' as in a story, a set of instructions or report of a business trip. With more advanced students who are used to the activity you can use other types of text with which they are familiar such as scientific papers or discursive arguments.
2 Split the text and write each part on a different index card.

Procedure

1 Shuffle your cards and read out the text in jumbled order. Read at normal speed, taking care not to deform normal intonation and rhythm.
2 Encourage students to take notes as they listen. Remind them it is not a dictation, so they shouldn't try to take down everything.
3 Ask students to work in groups of three or four. Pooling their notes, they work together to write out the reconstructed text as accurately as they can. This includes:
   ● filling in information using each other's notes.
   ● putting the information in the correct order.
   (NB If you use a news story from a newspaper or magazine, point out that in English journalists tends to start with the latest event and work backwards).
4 Ask each group to find a suitable title for the text.
5 Read the text out loud in the correct order so that students can compare their version to the original.

ONE-TO-ONE
1 Read out the text as described above.
2 Ask your student to take notes, concentrating only on the essential information.
3 Give some time for the student to organise their notes.
4 The student reads back their text to you and you note any significant information which is missing from their version.
5 Ask the student to turn their paper over. Read out bits of the text containing important missing facts or information. Meanwhile, the student takes notes.
6 Allow time for them to integrate the notes into their text.
7 The student re-reads their text to you.

8 You read out the original text in the correct order while your student compares the two texts.

NOTE

Steps 3 and 6 of the one-to-one procedure are important as they encourage student autonomy.

5.15

LEVEL
Intermediate+

MATERIALS
A pile of
advertisements
from a non-
English speaking
country, TV
commercials from
same country
(optional)

TIME
30 to 40 minutes

FOCUS
Discussion,
Making
hypotheses,
Predicting

ADVERTISEMENT STEREOTYPES

Many of our students are learning English as an *international* language. That is, they use English as a means of communication with people from countries where the native language is not English. They may need to learn about these non-English speaking cultures; looking at advertisements is a good way to do this.

Preparation

Find and cut out advertisements from a non-English speaking country. These can be taken from various sources: magazines, newspapers, video recordings.

Procedure

1 Make small groups and give each group a pile of advertisements to look at. If videoed advertisements are available, some groups can work with these while others work with the printed ads.
2 Ask students to look at each ad and decide:
   ● what product or service is being advertised.
   ● what information about the lifestyle and value system of the cultural group runs through the ads.
   ● what aspects of the 'national character' the ads appeal to. For example, thrift, seriousness, organisation, hardworking attitude, etc.
   ● what stereotypes are apparent in the ads.
3 Ask students to discuss how they can apply this knowledge in their contacts with people from this culture. Or ask them to discuss differences between this culture and their own.

NOTE
We recently taught a group of French engineers who are now working with a Swedish company following the merger of their two companies. English is their official language when the French and Swedes work together. Our French engineers wanted to know a little bit about what makes the Swedes tick. Looking at ads from Sweden was one of the activities we used. Students were soon able to pick up on the recurring stereotypes. They found out quite a bit about Swedish family life – for example, the more equal role of men and women, the Swedish love of nature and being outdoors and the use of brighter colours in home decoration. There was also a strong stereotype of the Swede being an intellectual, a lover of learning and of books. There was an emphasis on doing activities either individually or with the family unit rather than with friends. Students noticed differences in customs and holidays (e.g. Santa Lucia Day). All in all the activity gave students a good introduction to Sweden even though no one spoke any Swedish.

ONE-TO-ONE
You and your student exchange ads from your own countries and then each draw up a list of national and cultural stereotypes for discussion.

ACKNOWLEDGEMENT
The idea of using advertisements as a key to cultural stereotypes comes from *All's Well 2* (Dickinson, Leveque, Sagot, 1976).

JUMBLED UP TITLES

This activity encourages students to read newspapers, professional or current events magazines, or technical articles. It plays on the fact that headlines or titles are not always easily understood by the foreign reader.

Procedure

1 Everyone chooses an article to read. This is done at home or in class. It is important that students read individually.
2 Tell everyone to print the title of their article in block capital letters on an index card. Ask students to do this secretly and not look at each other's cards.
3 Collect the cards, shuffle them, and lay them out where everyone can read the titles.
4 Students form pairs and tell each other about their article without mentioning the title.
5 Afterwards, students go to the cards and identify the title of the story they heard about.
6 Students move on to a new partner.
7 This time they tell their partner the title of their article. Student A infers the content from the title and tells student B what they think it's about.
8 Student B listens and corrects only when necessary.
9 Pairs switch roles and repeat the activity.
10 Students then write a summary of their article or record it as a news bulletin.

ACKNOWLEDGEMENT
We learned this technique from Anne Dechin.

5.16

LEVEL
Intermediate

MATERIALS
A selection of articles adapted to the interest and level of the group, index cards

TIME
60 Minutes

FOCUS
Reading skills, Summarising, Predicting

5.17

LEVEL
Intermediate

MATERIALS
A vocabulary list
relating to a
written text or a
video

TIME
20 Minutes

FOCUS
Building
vocabulary,
Explaining

VOCABULARY, VOCABULARY

Getting students to learn and practise new vocabulary such as technical terms is not always fun. This very easy technique puts vocabulary learning in a more communicative form which gives oral practice as well.

Procedure

1 Give each student a copy of the vocabulary list.
2 Ask them to choose three terms they know the definition of and three they don't know.
3 Tell students to mingle and exchange their terms. They give out the definitions they know to the others and in return seek the definitions of their chosen three unknown terms.
4 Bring the group back together. Each student tells the class one new term and definition that they learned.
5 Ask if there were any terms that no one seemed to have the definition for. Write these terms up on the board and either give the definitions yourself or ask students to use a dictionary.

ACKNOWLEDGEMENT
Inspiration for this activity came from Mario Rinvolucri during a workshop in St. Etienne, France.

CHAPTER 6

Gathering information through listening

Business people have to listen to presentations, conversations, and discussions which may be long and demand extreme concentration. They also need to be able to put themselves in the other person's shoes so they can understand not only what that person is saying but why. Developing good listening comprehension is vital. It can make the difference between signing the contract or not. The activities in this chapter have the explicit objective of developing these skills of active, sustained, and empathetic listening through practice. They help students to develop strategies they can use outside the classroom.

THREE QUESTIONS

This simple activity works at all levels when you want to check comprehension and get students speaking about a video clip.

Procedure

1 Show the video clip once and ask students if they think they have understood most of what happened.
2 If the consensus is positive, ask everyone to write down three questions that they can answer about what they've seen and three questions that they can't. If the consensus is negative, play the clip a second time. You can reassure your students by reminding them that their questions can be about what they saw as well as what they heard. For example, *How many people were at the meeting?* or *What was the managing director wearing?* are fair questions if students feel stressed. As students gain confidence, they will automatically ask more questions about what they hear.
3 Students then ask and answer their questions in one large group. They will be surprised to find that they have understood a great deal, if not all, of the clip.
4 Play the clip again now so that students can verify their understanding. If your goals were global comprehension and an animated question/answer discussion period, stop here. Follow up with a practice/consolidation activity such as a role play.

6.1

LEVEL
Elementary+

MATERIALS
A one to five-minute long video clip

TIME
15 to 30 minutes

FOCUS
Asking and answering questions, Listening

5 If you are aiming for in-depth comprehension of the passage, you can help your students' comprehension by using the following techniques:

- Replay the unclear passage. Stop before or after the important information, and try to elicit it.
- Ask one student to stop the video after every sentence. One of the others in the group writes each sentence on the board.
- Write out the passage with gaps. Students fill them in.
- Write out sentences in jumbled order. Students put them in the right order.
- Give the students the transcript with a few discrepancies which they must tick as you replay the clip.
- Give the students a list of phrases. They note which person/ character says each phrase.

6 Always replay the tape a last time after using any of these techniques so that students can check their comprehension.

RATIONALE

Even if you have chosen a passage appropriate to the level of your group, students often take more notice of what they have *not* understood than what they *have*. In our experience, THREE QUESTIONS is one of the best ways to help students to realise that they have understood a lot even if they haven't got it all. Students feel reassured because there are always three questions they can answer. And very often the three questions that they can't answer can be answered by another student.

6.2

LEVEL
Intermediate

MATERIALS
Small paper squares

TIME
20 to 30 minutes

FOCUS
Basic tenses, Speaking and listening, Note-taking

LISTENING FOR FACTS

While giving students practice in the all-important skill of note-taking, this activity provides a structure for them to decide what they want to speak about. It recognises that business people and technicians do not always want to talk about their jobs. One nuclear engineer wanted to talk about flowers, holidays and the future!

Procedure

1 Give out three squares of paper to each student.
2 Students note down on each square of paper a very general topic that they or anyone could speak about for two minutes.
3 Collect the papers.
4 In turn each student draws a paper and speaks for two minutes on that topic. The rest of the group are listeners and write down all the facts they hear.
5 After each talk, listeners call out the facts they remember about that topic.

6 Provided interest is high, repeat the exercise until each student has spoken once or more.

ONE-TO-ONE
As above.

ACKNOWLEDGEMENT
This is a variation of an idea in *Vocabulary* (Morgan and Rinvolucri, 1986, p. 87).

YES, I AGREE

Procedure

1 Elicit agreeing/disagreeing phrases from your students. Then hand out photocopies of your prepared list to which they can add any of their phrases which are missing, or refer students to a list of phrases in their textbook.
2 Go over the phrases orally with the students to make sure they are familiar with them all.
3 Ask students to form pairs and say the phrases to each other to practise pronunciation and intonation. You walk among the pairs and provide help when you are asked or as you hear it's needed.
4 Tell the pairs that you are going to call out a topic and that student A will spontaneously give their opinions on this subject for two minutes. Topics can be quite business focused, for example performance related pay, smoking in the office, flexi-time, the role of trade unions. Or students may prefer to talk about social subjects such as vegetarianism, a political leader, Chinese food. Student B listens carefully, perhaps jotting down main ideas.
5 During the talks, you walk among the pairs and monitor to make sure that students are giving their opinions rather than telling facts.
6 Student B then has two minutes to tell the other student *point by point* if they agree or disagree with what they have just heard.
7 Repeat the activity three or four times with students A and B changing roles and/or changing partners. Circulate among the pairs, listen, and check that they are using the phrases on their lists; suggest they use one or two new phrases at each repetition of the activity.

VARIATION
To make the activity more challenging at higher levels, combine LISTENING FOR FACTS (6.2) and YES, I AGREE (6.3). Tell the speakers to give both facts and opinions. The listeners should mark an F (for fact) or O (for opinion) beside each idea in the notes they take.

ACKNOWLEDGEMENT
The inspiration for this activity came from an exercise in *Functions of American English* (Jones and van Baeyer, 1983).

6.3

LEVEL
Intermediate

MATERIALS
A list of useful agreeing/ disagreeing phrases, a list of subjects you think your students can give opinions about for at least two minutes

TIME
20 to 30 minutes

FOCUS
Agreeing and disagreeing, Speaking and listening

6.4

LEVEL
Intermediate+

MATERIALS
A five-minute text
or recording,
dozens of small
paper squares
(about note-pad
size)

TIME
45 minutes

FOCUS
Developing
listening
strategies

LISTENING SQUARES

This activity is excellent preparation for students who attend business meetings or seminars conducted in English. It simulates what happens at a lecture or conference where participants must listen and take notes at the same time. Try to choose a recording or text which is as close to what students are likely to find in their business life as possible.

Procedure

1 Ask students to listen while you play a 5-minute recording or read a text out loud.
2 Before a second listening give each student a pile of ten or fifteen paper squares for note-taking. They can write anything they wish, for example:
   ● a fact from the talk
   ● an opinion they have about something said
   ● some other idea triggered by what they heard, e.g. 'sounds like what my boss would say', 'that reminds me of our new model for export', etc.
   ● thoughts about the talk, e.g. 'funny voice – too fast for me', etc.
   ● vocabulary or expressions they hear or think of.
3 After this, or after an additional listening if really necessary, tell students to organise and display their paper squares on the table in a way which is meaningful to them and which they can later explain to the group. Some may organise facts in the order they heard them. Others will organise thematically. Others may make mind maps.
4 When they have finished laying out their papers, the students move around as if they were at an exhibition. They look at each others' displays and ask and answer questions about not only what they see written on the papers but the principles for organising the squares.
5 Bring the group back together, play/read the text a final time. Invite your students to draw conclusions about differences in how we listen, what we listen for and how we later organise information.

VARIATION
With lower level students, listen to a recorded text and fill in paper squares at the same time as they do. Then as a model organise your papers yourself or ask your students to do this.

RATIONALE

When students compare and discuss their organisation of their notes, they are generally surprised to find that they are all selective listeners who pick out different information and then organise it in a different way. They also realise that the organisation is affected by opinions and stray thoughts. This awareness can then help students to improve their listening skills.

EXAMPLE

In one group of six advanced students who had listened to a text, three had organised the information in the same order as the bits of information had occurred in the text. Of these three, the strongest had noted complete phrases, the two others only words. In comparing their notes they found that they had extracted basically the same information, but got into a discussion as to which facts or ideas were more interesting or useful to them personally. One student had noted down ideas he had heard in the text, but in no particular order. Another student noted down both ideas from the text and his own opinions on how to listen, sparking the group into a discussion about listening problems and solutions. And one student noted down nothing at all saying, 'I can't listen and take notes at the same time.' He had remembered a few ideas from the text, but by looking at the other students' notes realised that he had forgotten more than he remembered. This student became aware that he had to work on his note-taking skills if he wished to improve his comprehension. The group as a whole decided that listening for repeated words was a good way to focus their concentration. They found that taking notes of ideas in the order they heard them was the easiest to do.

ONE-TO-ONE

1 After listening, the student shows you their papers and explains their organisation to you.
2 You both discuss different listening strategies. Then you present alternatives such as use of key words or phrases, linear note-taking, mind maps, or listing their ideas sparked off by the text.
3 The student should then say which strategy they used during the first listening.
4 Ask the student to use a different strategy while listening to the same text.

6.5

LEVEL
Intermediate+

MATERIALS
A cassette player
for each pair of
students, a
cassette
recording of a
short (three-
minute) talk for
each pair of
students, a few
copies of two or
three other short
recorded talks

TIME
60 minutes

FOCUS
Developing
listening
comprehension
and awareness of
different listening
strategies

LISTENING STRATEGIES

This activity follows on from LISTENING SQUARES (6.4). It helps students to differentiate their listening strategies, which develops their autonomy as users of English.

Preparation

Choose three or four three-minute recorded talks of similar listening difficulty. The students are going to be predicting the content so the recordings need to be on subjects with which they are likely to be very familiar. Research shows the more you know about a topic the more you are likely to be able to predict. The best subjects will be either directly related to the students' business area or general topics which they know well, such as their own political system or the top news story of the moment.

Procedure

1 Put students in pairs and give them the title of the talk of which you have one recording for each pair. Tell them they will listen to the talk later.
2 Tell them to think about how they listen and to discuss and find different listening strategies. Typical listening strategies involve listening for:
   ● anything they notice
   ● facts relevant to their own work
   ● differences between what is on the cassette and their expectations, given the subject of the talk
   ● grammatical forms which they think might crop up
   ● vocabulary or expressions they might expect
   ● expressions that signal an opinion, e.g. 'I believe that . . .'
   ● figures, statistics, or technical terms
3 Listening strategies depend upon the kind of information heard in a talk. Ask them to think about the possible content of the talk based on the title you gave them in Step 1. They can write out lists, brainstorm, or make mind maps. Ask them what kinds of things they would listen for, given this content.
4 Give each pair of students a cassette player and a cassette with the chosen recorded talk.
5 Students in each pair agree on a listening strategy and try it out as they listen to their recording. They then choose other strategies and try them out as they re-listen to the same recording.

6 Give them the following questions to answer after their listenings:

Which information did you predict would be in the talk?
Which listening strategy did you choose first? Why?
Do you feel you gleaned enough information of the sort you wanted?
Which listening strategy did you choose next?
Which strategy was the most successful?
Can you say why?
How could you refine your strategies to make them more successful?
Would you add something?
Take something away?
Change something?

7 Give each pair one of the other recordings and its title and tell them that they are going to exchange listening strategies with another pair. Pair one suggests a listening strategy for pair two and vice versa. To do this, pairs first exchange recording titles and think about the possible content of each other's talks, following Step 3.

8 Pairs now listen to the new recordings and try out the suggested listening strategy.

9 Put the pairs who exchanged listening strategies together and ask them to talk about their impressions. Encourage discussion about the advantages and drawbacks of different strategies. When would they use different ones? Which ones have they used? Do some seem to be more 'universal' than others?

10 Bring the group back together for a general feedback session during which they draw up a list of listening strategies potentially useful in their work situations.

ONE-TO-ONE

1 With you the student discusses, predicts, chooses a strategy, listens and then relates what they have heard.

2 They then choose another strategy and compare it with the one tried first.

6.6

LEVEL
Elementary+

MATERIALS
A box of
Cuisenaire rods
for each six to
eight students

TIME
30 minutes

FOCUS
Listening/
Speaking,
Presentation skills

MY PLACE OF WORK

This is an easy activity which has proved popular with business people and professionals. If you haven't got any Cuisenaire rods you can use coloured pencils.

Procedure

1 Invite students to form a circle around you.
2 Place the rods in the centre of this circle where they can be easily seen. Use them one by one to construct a model of your place of work. You can add any details you wish – objects such as telephones, desks, computers or people such as your boss or colleagues. Don't speak while you are setting up your 'place'. Use the same colour of rod to represent the same thing in your model, e.g. red rods represent chairs and green ones desks.
3 Pointing to each colour of rod, say what it represents.
4 After you have finished your description, ask questions to check students' comprehension or ask students to ask you or each other questions.
5 Ask everyone to take the rods they need and go to different parts of the room where they construct their own place of work.
6 As a group, you and the class visit each 'exhibit'. Students take turns presenting their places of work. You and the other students ask questions.

VARIATIONS
These models are powerful images of your students' reality. Use them to provide vivid settings for role plays. For example, take a rod of a colour which has not been used and pretend that this rod walks in the door and asks either for information or to see one of the people in the office.

ONE-TO-ONE
Proceed as above.

NOTE
Cuisenaire rods are narrow rods of varying lengths and colours, named after Georges Cuisenaire, the educator who first used them. They are often used for teaching maths and with the Silent Way, a system for learning languages created by the late Caleb Gattegno. If you don't know about using these rods, MY PLACE OF WORK is one of the easiest exercises to start off with. After doing this exercise, you will see how the rods can be used to stimulate use of descriptive language.

Used in another way, rods encourage visualisation of language rather than scenes. For example, students associate the different lengths, colours and formation of rods with different words or different elements of a sentence. This aids both comprehension and memory. In our experience using the rods this way allows students to learn language which in more traditional approaches might seem too complex for their level of proficiency. An example of the use of rods to represent words follows in our next activity, JERUSALEM.

ACKNOWLEDGEMENT
For more on Cuisenaire rods, see *Images and Options in the Language Classroom* (Stevick, 1986).

JERUSALEM

6.7

This activity is easy to adapt to all levels from elementary up to very advanced by varying the difficulty of the descriptive language and the type of verbal participation you demand.

LEVEL
Elementary+

MATERIALS
A box of
Cuisenaire rods

Procedure

1 Bring the group together around a table or sit on the floor in a circle.
2 Place the rods in the centre where they can be easily seen and reached.
3 Start to describe an imaginary city or a real one which is unknown to the students.
4 For each landmark in the city lay down a Cuisenaire rod which represents what you are describing.
5 Continue until you have described all the different landmarks of the city and represented them with a rod.
6 Silently, point out the different landmarks. Invite students to call out the name.
7 Students point to different rods of the city and invite you to name them. Students generally like it if you pretend to become confused at this point and they can correct you.

TIME
45 minutes

FOCUS
Listening,
Speaking

Invite each student in turn to make a sentence about the city. You can help lower level students by using the rods to represent words.

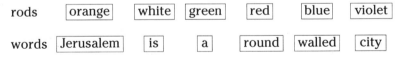

8 At this point, you can take the city apart piece by piece. Give rods representing landmarks to different students, who rebuild the city naming each part as they lay down the rods which represent it.
9 Ask the students to write a description of the city.
10 In pairs or groups, students build up and describe a city they know.

VARIATIONS

Besides cities, almost anything can be built up and described – factories, engines, aeroplanes, company organisation charts, etc.

We use the old city of Jerusalem as an example, because we know it well. In our experience students remember it months later.

NOTE

When dealing with elementary level students, be careful to use 'caretaker language', e.g.

- Use proper names. These will serve as signposts throughout the description.
- Use pauses to highlight important information.
- Repeat important information often (but always with natural intonation).
- Speak in a soft, low tone of voice but avoid a monotone – use a good range of pitch and stress important information.
- Use plenty of gesture and mime.

ACKNOWLEDGEMENT

Earl Stevick has written about a similar use of Cuisenaire rods in *A Way and Ways*, (1980, p. 139.)

LISTENER OR SPEAKER?

Procedure

6.8

LEVEL
Intermediate+

TIME
20 minutes

FOCUS
Fluency practice
in unrehearsed
speaking,
Listening skills

1 Ask students to think about themselves a bit and decide if they are more of a speaker or a listener. They write the answer to this question on a piece of paper and put it away for later use.
2 Students either sit or stand in two rows or concentric circles, face to face with a partner. Tell students that they are going to have two minutes to discuss a topic with the person opposite them. Here are some possible topics:

    my boss
    my route to work
    my favourite part of my job
    why I chose my profession
    the hardest part of my job
    the job I'd most like to do in my company
    my car
    watching TV
    writing letters
    an embarrassing experience
    a restaurant I enjoy

3 After two minutes, signal for the discussions to stop and for everyone to change partners.
4 Give a new topic. The new pairs speak for two minutes.
5 Continue in this way until everyone has spoken to everyone else or until you judge that the group is ready to stop.
6 Ask everyone to reconsider the question: 'Are you more a listener or a speaker?' and to look at the answer they wrote. Do they still agree?
7 Discuss which elements determined whether participants were listener or speaker each time.

VARIATION

1 Set up and focus a video camera before the group arrives. After several changes of partners, view the film and ask people to try to see who was a listener and who was a speaker and if they changed roles as they changed partners. Discussion can bring out people's reasons for changing roles.
2 If there is an odd number of participants, put an extra chair at the end of one of the rows and students take turns observing. Observers report their observations back to the group after several changes of partners.

RATIONALE

Most students believe they speak half of the time and listen half of the time. But during this activity they find out that talking and listening time depends on different factors (interest or knowledge of the topic, the personality and tendency of their partner, linguistic ability, lack of initiative or response from their partner, etc.). Although people recognise and accept the influence of these different factors when speaking in their own tongue, in a language they feel less confident with, they tend to think all communication problems come from their lack of linguistic knowledge. LISTENER OR SPEAKER helps students to see that this isn't so. This awareness helps them to prepare for everyday business situations in a foreign language.

ACKNOWLEDGEMENT
David Miller of ILTC Paris first showed us a variation of this activity when demonstrating how to train teachers to use a video camera.

6.9

LEVEL
Upper
Intermediate+

MATERIALS
A selection of art reproductions in a mixture of styles and periods and featuring strong central characters in a variety of surroundings, a recording of a piece of classical music

TIME
30 minutes

FOCUS
Listening and Speaking

INTO A PICTURE

For students used to very traditional language-learning techniques, this activity may well provide a new experience. It is very important that you as teacher feel comfortable with this activity otherwise your students will reject it. Before doing it in class, read it through carefully, visualising the steps in your mind. If you respond to the ideas here, your students will too.

Preparation

1 Before doing this activity, you should provide a model for the work to follow. Do this by leading a short relaxation exercise, for example, a multi-sensory guided visualisation. Students close their eyes, and with some classical baroque music as a background, you lead them on a walk through a garden where you invite them to visualise and admire the colours of the flowers, smell their lovely scents, touch the velvet of their petals, feel the breeze slowly waving the flowers from side to side, etc. (Alternatively, describe a painting or photo.)
2 Then, on each of two opposite walls of the room, place four to six art reproductions just before the activity begins.

Procedure

1 Form pairs of students, chairs side by side but each facing an opposite wall so that students are looking at the two walls where there are no pictures. This arrangement permits easy conversation between partners while hiding the pictures from their direct line of vision.
2 Partners go to the wall to their right and look at the pictures. They choose one and observe it closely. They concentrate on images in the picture and imagine what they could see, hear, touch, taste and

smell (for example flowers, perfume, food, etc.) if they were *in* the scene depicted. They imagine emotions they could feel. They pay special attention to colours, forms and positions.

3 Partners come back together and take turns speaking about and listening to each other's multi-sensory description of the picture. Time limit: two minutes for each partner.

4 Students return to their chosen picture and observe it again, but this time from the point of view of one of the characters shown.

5 Repeat Step 3, with students giving the same multi-sensory description but this time as the character in the picture speaking in the first person. Time limit: two minutes for each description.

6 Students go and find the picture they have heard described and observe it in the multi-sensory manner described in Step 2.

7 Pairs re-form and share their impressions about the pictures.

NOTE

Art is a powerful stimulus and some students will be very deeply touched by this activity. In general, we have found it works best with groups which have developed a strong sense of solidarity and confidence. We suggest the activity come towards the end of the lesson, when students feel a little tired. They participate in a different sort of experience and go home savouring the lovely sensations this activity provokes. We use this activity in training professional people in negotiation and team-building where it is important to know what other people are feeling and at the same time be able to talk about one's own feelings.

ONE-TO-ONE

Proceed as above.

This is a very powerful activity which brings you and your student closer on a personal level.

ACKNOWLEDGEMENT

June Mac Ostrich showed us this technique at Pilgrims, Canterbury, in August 1990.

6.10

FOLLOW MY INSTRUCTIONS

This activity works best with people who work with graphics (e.g. technicians, engineers, and designers) and who therefore need to give and understand clear and concise instructions.

Procedure

1 Ask for two volunteers. Give student A a picture which student B cannot see.
2 Explain to the group that student A will give instructions to student B as to how to draw the picture. Meanwhile, the rest of the group will stand so that they can see both student A's picture and student B's drawing.
3 Ask the group of observers to take notes as they watch what happens. Criteria for observation are:
   ● Were the instructions clear?
   ● Where were they unclear?
   ● What did student B do when the instructions were unclear?
   ● What could student A have said to make their instructions clearer and easier to follow?
4 When student A and B have finished, hold a feedback session.
   ● First ask student A how they felt while giving the instructions: what was easy to explain and what was difficult?
   ● Next ask student B how they felt when following the instructions: what was easy to understand and what was difficult, and why?
   ● Ask observers to report.

VARIATION
After doing this as a group exercise, split the group into threes and repeat the activity with students A and B as above and student C as observer.

ONE-TO-ONE
1 The student gives the instructions to you.
2 Once the drawing is complete, you both note down your feelings as in Step 6 above.
3 Have a feedback session and compare your feelings based on your notes.

ONE-TO-ONE VARIATION
Recording the drawing session can be very helpful as students can go back and listen to their own instructions.

THE VISITOR

Most teachers of a foreign language have visitors from time to time who are native speakers of the target language. It seems a shame to not bring them into class.

Procedure

STAGE ONE

1 Without giving too many details, tell your students that you have a visitor.
2 Ask them to draw up a list of questions to ask your visitor. Give them ten minutes and have them write the questions down.
3 Students tape record their questions. On the recording, students introduce themselves and each ask one or more of their questions.
4 Play the recording so the students can listen to themselves and their questions.

STAGE TWO

5 Play the tape of questions to your visitor and record their answers. You will need two tape recorders to do this – one to play the questions and the other to record the questions off the first machine as well as your visitor's answers.
6 Take the finished question/answer tape back to class and play it for your students.

6.11

LEVEL
Elementary+

MATERIALS
A visitor, two cassette players, and two empty cassettes

TIME
20 minutes for each stage

FOCUS
Asking questions and listening

USES OF THE NEWS

Access to a news broadcast in English is usually easy to get. Using authentic news broadcasts trains students how to listen selectively in a variety of real life situations.

Preparation

Record a news summary or some selected news stories from a longer broadcast. The recording should be three to five minutes in length. For lower levels, prepare an easier worksheet than the example provided; include a checklist of people and places mentioned in the recording.

Procedure

1 Split your class into small listening groups.
2 Give each group a cassette player, a recording of the news and a copy of the News Worksheet for each student (see page 110).
3 Tell students that they have twenty minutes to complete the worksheet.
4 In plenary, students discuss and compare their answers.

6.12

LEVEL
Lower intermediate+

MATERIALS
An authentic recording of the news in English, a photocopy of News Worksheet for each student

TIME
30 minutes

FOCUS
Listening skills

EXTENSION

Students compare the news broadcast with an account in a news-paper. They should:

● Underline information heard in the news broadcast.
● Find any discrepancies.
● Look for new facts.

ONE-TO-ONE

1 Ask your student to record the news in English and bring it to class the next day.
2 Both of you listen and complete the worksheet in class.
3 Together you discuss and compare answers.

ONE-TO-ONE VARIATION

A student on a short intensive course can keep a listening diary of the news every day over the duration of the course. As their listening comprehension increases, they become aware of progress over a short period of time.

News worksheet for Activity 6.12

1 Listen to the news broadcast and count the number of stories.
2 Listen and write the subject of each news story beside the category it belongs to:
   – politics
   – economy
   – sports
   – human interest
   – disaster
   – crime
   – other
3 Listen and write down all the names of people and places.
4 Write down all the numbers and figures you hear.
   – how much money?
   – how many people?
   – what percentages?
   – what dates?
   – what time?
   – other?
5 Write a headline for each story.
6 Choose one story and write a short summary. In your summary make sure you answer these questions:
   – who is it about?
   – when did it happen?
   – where did it happen?
   – what exactly happened?

LISTENING TO DISCOURSE
Procedure

STAGE ONE

1 Split your class up into small listening groups. Give each group a cassette player.

2 Provide each group with a recorded authentic text. Use either a short monologue or a dialogue. Give out short texts the first few times you do this activity, but progressively use longer and longer selections.

3 Before the class begins listening, preview the text using drawing or pictures or describe the scene.

4 Encourage students to predict the content of the discourse. They guess what the speaker(s) might say in this situation.

5 Give students control of the cassette players and ask them to listen carefully and discuss what they hear on the cassette. You walk round and monitor what they are doing. Encourage them to stop the tape from time to time and ask and answer the following questions:

● What could the speaker say next, given the context?

● What do they then actually say?

● Can you understand and repeat what they are saying?

● And now, what could they say next?

STAGE TWO

6 Invite a native speaker to class and ask them to speak to the class on any subject of their choice.

7 Ask students to keep notes on:

● How the speaker uses eye contact.

● How the speaker uses space.

● Relationships between gestures and what they are saying.

● Expressions or noises the speaker makes when hesitating. (e.g. 'Well then . . .', 'Right . . .', 'Uhhh . . .', 'Mmm . . .', 'OK . . .' etc.)

● Expressions the speaker uses to link their ideas together. (e.g. 'next . . .', 'before I go on . . .', 'at this point . . .', 'firstly . . .', 'finally . . .', 'to sum up . . .', etc.)

● Words or expressions the speaker uses which the student wouldn't use.

STAGE THREE

8 Students discuss and compare notes taken during the native speaker's talk.

STAGE FOUR

9 Ask students to form pairs.

6.13

LEVEL
Elementary+

MATERIALS
Listening material and cassette players

TIME
30 minutes for each stage

FOCUS
Listening skills

10 Student A talks about something of interest for three minutes. Student B listens and notes down expressions which break up or link student A's talk. (e.g. 'Well then . . .', 'Right . . .', 'Uhhh . . .', 'Mmm . . .', 'OK, . . .' 'next . . .', 'before I go on . . .', 'at this point . . .', 'firstly . . .', 'finally . . .', 'to sum up . . .', etc.)

11 Students A and B change roles and student B talks while student A notes down expressions.

12 With higher level classes pairs then work together to create a flow chart or diagram of the talks, showing how the expressions noted served to link or break up the discourse.

STAGE FIVE

13 Invite another native speaker to class, or tell a story.

14 Ask the class to make notes as in Step 7, then discuss and compare notes in pairs and create another flow chart.

CHAPTER 7

Business strategies

This chapter is about negotiation, team building, problem-solving, decision making, and other management activities. Many of the activities used in business schools fit nicely into the kind of language training professional people need and enjoy. Use activities in this chapter when your class has come together as a group and the students are confident enough to work on their own. Students learn through working things out for themselves in largely 'teacherless' tasks. They apply their English to situations similar to those they find in their jobs.

GUESS MY OBJECT

Technical language can involve describing objects with great precision. This activity gives practice in deciphering as well as in asking questions.

Procedure

1 Give each student a photocopy of the worksheet (see page 115).
2 Each student in turn reads out and then mimes or explains the vocabulary in one of the ten sentences of Part One on the worksheet. Help whenever necessary.
3 Tell students that you have a completed grid (see Fig. 13). Add that they can fill in the empty grids (Fig. 14) in Part Two of the worksheet by asking you yes/no questions. For example: *Is the wrench small? Is it long?* Tell students that in reality many of the characteristics of the tools are not mutually exclusive, but for the purposes of the exercise they are being treated as such. With regard to colour, point out that the four objects can come in different colours but that you are thinking of a particular colour for each one.
4 As students receive answers, they all fill in their grids. Tell them that when someone has all of the characteristics for one tool, they should read these out loud to see if everyone else agrees.
5 After the first tool has been described in this way, point out that the order of the words is important. When describing objects you usually do it in this order: size, colour, other qualifying adjectives, name of the object, relative clauses.

7.1

LEVEL
Elementary+

MATERIALS
A photocopy of the Guess my Object worksheet for each student

TIME
30 minutes

FOCUS
Word order when describing objects, Asking questions

6 When the grids are complete, students working in pairs complete the sentences in Part Three and read out the descriptions to each other.

7 Invite students to make up descriptions of their own using the models they now have. Other students try to guess the names of the tools or objects they are describing.

ONE-TO-ONE
As above.

ANSWER TABLE – GUESS MY OBJECT

	WRENCH	SPATULA	TONGS	SPADE
SIZE	30-centimetre	small	large	1.2-metre
COLOUR	grey	white	black	red
QUALIFIER 1	hand-held	flat	two-part	hard
QUALIFIER 2	metal	rubber	scissor-like	blunt
OBJECT	tool	utensil	instrument	implement
WHERE	workshop	kitchen	laboratory	garden
USE	holding and turning	spreading and mixing	gripping and holding	digging and breaking up

Fig. 13

1 This wrench is a 30-centimetre, grey, hand-held, metal tool which is used in the workshop for holding and turning.

2 This spatula is a small, white, flat, rubber utensil which is used in the kitchen for spreading and mixing.

3 These tongs are a large, black, two-part, scissor-like instrument which is used in the laboratory for gripping and holding.

4 This spade is a 1.2-metre, red, hard, blunt implement which is used in the garden for digging and breaking up earth.

WORKSHEET FOR ACTIVITY 7.1
Guess my object

PART ONE – CHARACTERISTICS: Read these sentences out loud.
1 There are four different objects: a wrench, a spatula, a spade and tongs.
2 They are used for digging, turning, mixing, spreading, holding, gripping, and breaking up.
3 One is thirty centimetres long, one is small, one large, and one 1.2 metres long.
4 Each is a different colour: black, white, grey, or red.
5 One is hard, one is hand-held, one is two-part, and one flat.
6 They are also rubber, scissor-like, metal, and blunt.
7 One is *generally* considered to be a tool, another an instrument, another a utensil, and the last an implement.
8 They are used in the kitchen, the workshop, the garden, and the laboratory.
9 The one used in the kitchen is made of rubber.
10 One of them is large and black.

PART TWO – GRID: Ask your teacher questions which can be answered by yes or no to help you fill in this grid.

	WRENCH	SPATULA	TONGS	SPADE
SIZE		small		
COLOUR				
QUALIFIER 1			two-part	
QUALIFIER 2				
OBJECT	tool			
WHERE				
USE				digging and breaking up

Fig. 14

PART THREE – SENTENCES: Complete these sentences when you have found the information.
1 This . . . is a . . . . . ., . . ., ..., ... which is used in the . . . for . . . and . . . . .
2 This . . . is a . . ., . . ., . . ., ...which is used in the . . . for . . . and . . . . .
3 These . . . are a . . ., . . ., . . ., ...,. . . which are used in the . . . for . . . and . . . . .
4 This . . . is a . . . . . ., . . ., . . ., ... which is used in the . . . for . . . and . . . . . . earth.

7.2

LEVEL
Elementary+

MATERIAL
A box of
Cuisenaire rods

TIME
15 to 20 minutes

FOCUS
First conditionals,
Negotiation
practice

IT'S A DEAL

Lower level students must practise the structures they need for negotiation. By negotiating among themselves, students gain confidence
for the real-life venture. If you haven't got any Cuisenaire rods, you
can use coloured pencils.

Procedure

1 With a box of rods in hand, go around to each student. Ask them
which rods they like best.
2 Tell each student that you will give them some rods of their choice,
if they do a simple task for you. For example:

You: Stephan, which rods do you like?
Stephan: I like the long black ones and the small light-green ones.
You: Okay. Well, I'll give you three long black rods and four small light-
green ones if you can count from fifty to one backwards in sixty
seconds.

3 The student does the task and you give them the rods.
4 Continue in this way around the group giving a short task to each
person.
5 When everyone has their rods, ask everyone to try to get more rods
by negotiating swaps. Give them an example like this:

Student A: Hello, if you give me one of your blue ones and four of your small
red ones, I'll give you one of my long black rods and two of my
light-green ones.
Student B: No, that's too many, but I'll give you one of my long blue ones
and two of my short red ones for one long black rod and two of
your small light-green ones.
Student A: Okay, it's a deal!

6 When noise and interest level is at its highest, stop the group. The
person with the most rods is the winner.

VARIATION
To spice up the game you can give secret arbitrary values to the
rods. When the final count is made, there's a surprise result for
everyone!

ONE-TO-ONE
1 Give your student a pile of rods of various colours and lengths.
2 Ask them to prepare some challenging general knowledge questions for you to answer. This is the student's chance to catch you
out! If you answer the question correctly, you get the rod(s). If you
don't, the student keeps them. The winner is the one with the most
rods at the end of the questions.

3 Your student starts by saying: 'I'll give you X rods if you can answer my question.'

4 They ask you all their questions.

5 Count up the rods together to see who has the most.

NOTE

Cuisenaire rods are perfect here because their different colours and lengths suggest different values.

NEGOTIATION GAME

7.3

This activity is a good starter for negotiation work because it makes students aware of strategies used during negotiations. If students are not experienced negotiators, before they start ask them to write down a cost price for the object (a price below which they would lose money by selling it) and an asking price (a high price which they do not expect to get but which is a basis for negotiation). They do not show these prices to the other students. In Step 4 students then compare the final price with the asking price and the cost price. Was the asking price too high/low? How near was the final price to the cost price, i.e. what was their profit margin?

LEVEL
Intermediate

MATERIALS
Small interesting or unusual objects, play money (optional)

TIME
20 minutes

FOCUS
Persuading and negotiating

Preparation

1 Ask students to each bring in one small object to sell, or bring some in yourself.

2 Provide play money.

Procedure

1 Make sure everyone has a small object. Distribute the play money.

2 Students circulate, looking at and asking questions about each other's objects for two or three minutes.

3 They then form pairs. Student A has five minutes to sell their object to student B at the highest possible price. After about five minutes tell the pairs to stop negotiating and change roles. Student B now has five minutes to sell their object to A.

4 When the negotiating is finished, ask each pair to analyse the steps they took in their negotiations. This can take the form of a flow chart, a table, or a list of dos and don'ts for a successful negotiation.

5 Ask each pair to report their steps to the group as a whole.

VARIATION

In multi-national groups it is interesting to make a list of cultural differences in approaching negotiation.

ACKNOWLEDGEMENT
This activity originated with Tony Parsons at Lancaster University.

7.4

LEVEL
Intermediate+

MATERIALS
Negotiation
Tactics
worksheets for
teams A and B

TIME
45 minutes

FOCUS
Persuading and
negotiating

NEGOTIATION LOOP

Procedure

1 Divide the class into equal numbers of small negotiating teams. Name each team A or B and pair every A team to a B team.
2 Give everyone a copy of a Negotiation Tactics worksheet (see page 119): A sheets to A people, B sheets to B people. Each sheet lists twelve tactics: Four are elements of a good negotiation, four are elements of a bad negotiation, and four can be good or bad depending on the culture or the situation. The tactics on the two lists are different but slightly overlap.
3 Ask students to read through the twelve tactics on the lists.
4 Each team then has fifteen minutes to discuss and negotiate a ranking (most important to least important) for the *seven* tactics they feel most essential to a successful negotiation. Each student should note down their team's ranking.
5 Form new teams by mixing members from groups A and B.
6 With each student using their top seven tactics (from Step 4), the new teams have fifteen minutes to negotiate a final ranked list of *six* essential tactics.
7 Each team presents their list to the class.
8 A last negotiation can take place between you and the teams to ensure that a list doesn't contain any undesirable tactics. For example: 'Defend and attack are your key words' wouldn't be desirable in most negotiations.

VARIATION

Advanced groups prepare their own negotiation lists of twelve tactics: four good, four bad, and four that are good or bad depending on the culture or the situation. A and B groups exchange their lists and proceed to Step Three.

ACKNOWLEDGEMENT
The idea of 'looping' negotiation skills grew out of a staffroom conversation between Tessa Woodward and one of the authors in the summer of 1988 (see Woodward, 1990).

WORKSHEET FOR ACTIVITY 7.4

Negotiation tactics

TEAM A

1 Establish rapport with the other negotiating team.
2 Consider the other party's proposal as one of the many options available.
3 Remember: it is always important to feel that you have won the negotiation.
4 Don't hesitate to use insults and irritators, in business everything is fair.
5 Explicitly label questions and suggestions: 'Let me offer a suggestion . . .' or 'Let me ask you a question . . .'.
6 Remain flexible as to options.
7 Only give a few reasons as to why you want something.
8 Do not drink during a negotiation; it affects your judgement and speed of thought.
9 Successful negotiators talk about their feelings and thoughts.
10 If you get stuck on a negotiation, try a different strategy.
11 Make a plan of the meeting and keep to it.
12 Consider that you are in the best position to win the negotiation.

TEAM B

1 Be alert – use your eyes, ears, and intuitions when negotiating.
2 *Defend* and *attack* are your key words.
3 Do not oversell your point of view.
4 Validate any proposal the other side makes by saying things like: 'That's a very good point.' or 'If I were in your shoes, that would be important to me.'
5 Be calm and develop good rapport with the other team.
6 Never negotiate with someone who doesn't have the power to make a decision.
7 State your reasons for making a proposal, then make the proposal.
8 Emphasise areas of agreement.
9 Show your true feelings during a negotiation by using expressions like, 'I'm feeling . . .'.
10 Ask for time out if you need to think about some new option which has arisen.
11 Keep in mind the importance of coming to an agreement.
12 If you need to reach an agreement quickly, you can always try to rush the other team.

7.5

LEVEL
Lower
Intermediate+

MATERIALS
Coloured felt pens
and paper

TIME
30 minutes

FOCUS
Adjectives which
describe
personality
characteristics,
Persuading and
convincing

YOUR ADVERTISEMENT

Advertisements influence the consumer to buy. In order to do this, advertisers must imagine what will appeal to the consumer.

Procedure

1 Start up a discussion about people and advertising. Bring up or elicit the following:
   - Different ads appeal to different kinds of people.
   - Ads often imply more than they explicitly say.
   - They usually create a fantasy around a product.
   - Ads use lots of adjectives to describe people and products.
   - Ads sell benefits not features; in other words they tell the consumer how the product will help them.
   - Ads often make an appeal to the heart and the head, i.e. to the emotions and to logic.
2 Put students in pairs that know each other well.
3 Tell students to think of a product that their partner might commonly use and to create an ad to promote it. Before making the ad, students should write adjectives on the back of the paper which describe the personality of their partner.
4 Students present their ads to each other first without showing the personality description. Each student tells their partner whether they would buy the product intended for them and tells how the ad appeals to them personally.
5 Students then show their adjectives to their partners and discuss the accuracy of these adjectives and the extent to which the ads appeal to these characteristics.

RATIONALE
Being able to create an ad successfully is excellent practice for business people who need to influence, persuade and convince others in their work.

IMAGE WATCHES
Procedure

7.6

LEVEL
Intermediate+

MATERIALS
For the variation:
Image Watch
advertisement

TIME
30 minutes

FOCUS
Problem-solving

1 Ask if anyone ever bets on horses. Ask if anyone can explain what the odds ten-to-seven mean. Discuss these questions:
   - If you bet ten dollars on a horse and it wins, what happens? What if you do the same and the horse loses?
   - If you owned your own business, would you prefer growth or shrinkage? Under what circumstances, if any, would you be satisfied with a standstill?

2 Split your class into groups of three or four. Tell each group to imagine that they own a business called 'Image Watches, Inc.'. Say that you will tell them some facts about their company and they should listen, take notes, and pool the information they've noted down. Read out the following:
   - Image Watches, Inc. has been the leader in logo watches for over ten years.
   - Ten years ago they developed a process to reproduce colour logos quickly and inexpensively.
   - With this process, they were the first to introduce low-cost logo watches to the international business community.
   - Their unique direct marketing method and the quality of their watches helped to establish a marketplace.
   - But they attribute most of their success to their self-imposed high standards in customer service which include: An unconditional money-back guarantee, consistent on-time ten-day delivery (sooner if needed), an offer to re-do any job at no cost to the customer until it meets with complete satisfaction.

3 Tell the groups to imagine they have a rich uncle in America who has just died and left them one hundred and fifty thousand dollars. They want to invest this money in their business: Image Watches, Inc. Ask them to discuss and decide where they will invest this money and why:
   - in working capital (raw materials, advertising, marketing, etc.)
   - in fixed assets (buildings, machinery, etc.)
   - in outside investments (money market, foreign currency, stocks, etc.)

(Some students may want to know the size of the company, i.e. capital, turnover and costs. Choose any figures you like for these – a plausible ratio is 1:10:6).

4 Each group reports where they have decided to invest their money and explains their reasons why.

5 Now tell everybody that next to their logo watch plant they own an empty lot which is a part of their fixed assets. It is worth a lot of money and they have had some interesting offers to buy it. Would they agree to sell? Students discuss this in groups, report and compare decisions.

VARIATION

Instead of orally giving out the information about Image Watches you can give a photocopy of the advertisement in Fig. 15 to each group and ask them to read and note down the principal facts about the company including why it is successful.

NOTE

Image Watches, Inc. exists. It is at 227 East Pomona Boulevard, Monterey Park, California 91754.

ACKNOWLEDGEMENT

Ken Kasler of the European School of Business Management, Paris, France used the example of betting on horses to introduce the concept of company investment.

WORKSHEET FOR ACTIVITY 7.6

Fig. 15

To get a good idea of what a great idea we have in Image Watches ... paste your color logo here.

THE LEADER IN LOGO WATCHES FOR OVER 10 YEARS!

Over twelve years ago Image Watches developed a process to reproduce color logos quickly and inexpensively. With this process we were the first to introduce logo watch samples to the American business community at very little cost, Allowing the customer to "try before you buy".

Our unique direct marketing method and the quality of our watches helped us to establish a marketplace. However, we attribute most of our success to our self-imposed high standards in customer service which includes:

1. An Iron-clad Unconditional Money-Back Guarantee, if not satisfied.
2. Consistent on time 10-day delivery service, sooner if needed.
3. Our offer to re-do any job until it meets with the customer's satisfaction – without cost to the customer.

In the true spirit of American business competition we invite customers to compare prices, the quality of watches, logo reproduction, on time delivery records, guarantees, and especially the during and after sales services. All logo watchmakers are NOT the same.

We are confident that our knowledge and experience in watchmaking and watch dial making, our commitment to customer services, and our longstanding reputation of quality will continue to guarantee our position as the leader of the logo watch industry.

OR EVEN BETTER
Send us your color logo

(Any size letterhead, photo, brochure, artwork. Complete logo design preferable.)

along with U.S. **$16.50 ea.** (Tax, Shipping included) **and we'll rush you a personalized working *quartz* watch sample as our convincer!**

Limit 2 samples per company @ $16.50 each

Your company logo in full color is the dial of a handsome wristwatch. Gold plated case, genuine leather band, battery powered quartz movement with 1 year limited warranty. Men's and women's sizes. Remarkably inexpensive even in **small quantities.**

A timely idea for –
- **Incentive**
- **Premium**
- **Dealer/Loader**
- **Business Gift**
- **Convention or Meeting Giveaway**

Catalog sheet and details on request.

(213) 726-8050
9 am - 5 pm Mon. - Fri.
Pacific Coast Time

IMAGE™ WATCHES, INC.
227 East Pomona Boulevard
Monterey Park, CA 91754

Attn: Mr. Errol

© Image ™ Watches, Inc.
all rights reserved

Unconditional Money Back Guarantee

7.7

LEVEL
Intermediate+

MATERIALS
Oracle's
Statements sheet

TIME
30 minutes

FOCUS
Question
formation,
Decision making

THE ORACLE

This activity takes students into a world where questions need to be clear if answers are to have meaning. 'The Oracle's' statements work rather like a master's koan in Zen. Students gain new insight into their questions rather than simply receiving pat answers as in traditional questionnaire activities.

Procedure

1 Remind students of how an oracle works: an oracle always gives an unclear answer to a question and a seeker must interpret this answer. Say that some of the class will be seekers. They must put questions to the oracles. Others in the group are oracles. They answer the questions. Remind them that each answer should be so mysterious that the seeker is left with a lot of thinking to do.

2 Form groups of six to eight. Then, divide these groups into halves. One half are 'oracles' and the other half are 'seekers'.

3 Give oracles their statement sheets to read (see page 125). Ask them to silently read the statements and, if they wish, add one or two more of their own, keeping to the spirit of the other statements. Tell them that they will use these statements to answer the seekers' questions.

4 Ask seekers to prepare questions about any aspect of their jobs or businesses which they would like to ask the oracles, e.g. 'Will I be made redundant?' Have them write these questions out.

5 Bring the two halves of each group together. Pair up seekers and oracles. Seekers ask their questions and oracles reply using what they feel are the best responses from their lists.

6 Seekers note down oracles' replies. For further clarification, seekers can ask one additional question but oracles use only their oracle's statement sheet to find the answer to this new question.

7 Form new pairs. They then discuss the meaning of the oracles' answers.

ACKNOWLEDGEMENTS
The original 'oracle' activity can be found in *Drama Techniques in Foreign Language Teaching* (Maley and Duff, 1978).

The statements on the oracle's sheet are from *Tigers Don't Eat Grass* (Jenkins, 1989).

WORKSHEET FOR ACTIVITY 7.7

Oracle's statements

Once one occupies oneself with the big, one loses interest in the small.

When two persons are in charge of a horse, it is bound to get thin.

Questions are never indiscreet but answers sometimes are.

Monetary policy is like a string: you can pull it through with incalculable results, but you cannot shove it at all.

Changing jobs is to jump to another trough.

Ten excuses are less persuasive than one.

Those who cannot sing can still be experts on singing.

The learning for which you pay will be remembered longer.

He who has failed three times, sets up as an instructor.

When the wind is great, bow before it; when the rain is heavy, yield to it.

It is wise to look ahead; but foolish to look further than you can see.

You say one thing, he understands three things.

Tigers don't eat grass.

Treat thy subordinates with kindness, thy equals with justice, and thy superiors with prudence.

Money speaks sense in a language all nations understand.

You must steer the rudder according to the wind.

If the profits are great, the risks are great.

The shortest way to do many things is to do only one thing at a time.

It is the politest pig that loses his place at the trough.

Rock stands, and mud washes away.

Each trade has its own ways.

To open a business is easy; the difficult thing is to keep it open.

A wise man leaves little to chance.

THREE PEOPLE IN A TUB

Business people enjoy playing games in class. More often than not, their professional training included games, case studies, and simulations. Their games, however, often involve solving practical and financial problems. In the following game, which is actually used in professional management training, we ask them to deal with human problems.

Procedure

1 Present the following situation to the group:

The people listed below are passengers on a ship which is sinking rapidly. The boat is in an isolated part of the world where there is little sea or air traffic. There is one lifeboat which will carry three people to a deserted island which can be seen in the distance. There is only time to save the three people who can fit in the boat. Which ones should be saved?

7.8

LEVEL
Intermediate+

MATERIALS
None

TIME
60 Minutes

FOCUS
Discussion,
Comparatives and
superlatives

a religious leader (priest, rabbi, etc.)	a postman
a housewife	a lawyer
a car salesman	a dancer
a waitress	a surfer
an unmarried, pregnant mother-to-be	a farmer
a firefighter	a grandmother
a former American president	a policeman

Ask students to choose their three survivors and be prepared to explain their choices. Give them twenty minutes.

2 Students mingle and tell each other their list of survivors.

3 Tell students to form small groups with other students who have chosen to save the same people. Ask them to explain their reasons to the whole group.

NOTE

One group decided to take the unmarried mother because it was a way of taking along an extra person and she could also be expected to have other children. They took the farmer because he would know how to cultivate plants and look after animals and because farmers have a lot of practical knowledge about weather, climate, medicine, etc. Finally, the surfer was saved because he knew about the ocean and tides, which would be an important part of their lives. Also surfers are normally quite young and in good physical condition which would increase chances of survival. Some more technically-minded students in our classes have turned the problem around and tried to see how the lifeboat could be used to save everyone!

ONE-TO-ONE

1 Ask your student to make a list of positions in the company from managing director to janitors and security guards, etc.

2 Ask your student to imagine that the company has experienced a disaster of some kind, and to choose the three survivors who would best be able to help the company carry on.

WHAT'S IMPORTANT?

We have found that this activity works especially well in groups where there are both managers and employees or where there are considerable age differences. It is from these contrasts that the most exciting discussion arises.

Procedure

1 Write up on the board or dictate the following list of job criteria:

   A. JOB SECURITY
   B. FULL APPRECIATION FOR WORK DONE
   C. PROMOTION AND GROWTH WITHIN A COMPANY
   D. TACTFUL DISCIPLINE
   E. GOOD WAGES
   F. FEELING 'IN' ON THINGS
   G. INTERESTING AND MEANINGFUL WORK
   H. MANAGEMENT LOYALTY TO WORKERS
   I. GOOD WORKING CONDITIONS
   J. SYMPATHETIC UNDERSTANDING OF PERSONAL PROBLEMS

2 Ask students to rank them from one to ten in the order of their importance (one being the top):
   a from a worker's point of view
   b from a manager's point of view
   c from their own personal point of view
   Each student will have three ranked lists.

3 In pairs or small groups students compare their rankings.

4 Bring the group back together for discussion. Below is the ranking most commonly found.

CRITERIA	RANKING FOR: MANAGERS	WORKERS
A. JOB SECURITY	2	4
B. FULL APPRECIATION FOR WORK DONE	8	1
C. PROMOTION AND GROWTH WITHIN A COMPANY	3	7
D. TACTFUL DISCIPLINE	7	10
E. GOOD WAGES	1	5
F. FEELING 'IN' ON THINGS	10	2
G. INTERESTING AND MEANINGFUL WORK	5	6
H. MANAGEMENT LOYALTY TO WORKERS	6	8
I. GOOD WORKING CONDITIONS	4	9
J. SYMPATHETIC UNDERSTANDING OF PERSONAL PROBLEMS	9	3

7.9

LEVEL
Intermediate+

MATERIALS
None

TIME
20 minutes

FOCUS
Comparatives,
Superlatives

VARIATION

1 After doing Step 1, divide the group into managers and employees.
2 Ask students to rank the job criteria. The manager group ranks from a manager's point of view and the employee group from an employee's point of view.
3 Form pairs of one manager and one employee who compare and discuss their rank orders.
4 Bring the group back together for discussion.

ONE-TO-ONE

This activity can be used to 'people' a one-to-one lesson.

1 Rank the criteria in order of importance for
   a an employee (if your student is a manager)
   b a manager (if your student is an employee)
   c a business colleague
   d someone from a different country.
2 Discussion and comparison as above.

7.10

LEVEL
Intermediate+

MATERIALS
Some Guidelines sheet for each group

TIME
60 minutes

FOCUS
Problem-solving and presentation skills

SO YOU'RE STARTING A NEW BUSINESS

Procedure

1 Split your class into groups of three to five students and tell them that each group is going to create their own company. They must decide what sort of company it will be.
2 Give each group the Some Guidelines sheet (see page 129).
3 Tell them that they can use the guidelines, but that they are also free to deviate from them or to ignore them. The guidelines are a gentle nudge into action and nothing more.
4 Tell groups that they have a time limit of thirty minutes. Ask them to make careful notes of all discussion so that they can present their company to the group.
5 When time is up, each group presents 'their company'.

VARIATION

This activity can be a project throughout an intensive course. In that case, give students some time each day to work on it. At the end of the course, ask each group to present their project orally. Encourage them, however, to produce visuals like layouts, diagrams, charts, drawings or written reports or brochures on the project. This gives everyone in the group a greater chance to participate. In larger groups (over fifteen), create small groups around different aspects of setting up a company: legal, financial, organisation, personnel, layout and design.

WORKSHEET FOR ACTIVITY 7.10

Some guidelines

1 Will you produce a product or offer a service?
2 Does an example of this sort of company already exist?
3 How large will your company be?
4 What provisions will be made for staffing?
5 What will be the hierarchy of the staff?
6 What will be your priorities when you choose your staff? Their educational and social background? Their experience?
7 What training will they get? What criteria will be used for selection?
8 What provision will be made for financing?
9 What legal status will you give your company?
10 What kind of buildings and environment do you wish for your company?
11 What sort of atmosphere do you wish to create?
12 Do you have a particular geographical location in mind?
13 What about equipment, furniture, special effects, etc.?
14 Do you have any special requirements about these, e.g. forms, shapes, colours?
15 How will decisions be made?
16 Who decides company policy?
17 What kind of words would you wish to use in an advertisement or company brochure?
18 What words would you leave out?
19 What would you say to convince the bank to finance your company?
20 What would you say to someone who says your company won't work?

© Longman Group Ltd. 1995 `Photocopiable`

AMERICAN IDEAS

Quite a few of our students work for American multinational companies or for companies which are trying to break into the American market. This activity is used in training American managers. While practising speaking and writing, students can gain insight into American-type group awareness and problem-solving.

Procedure

1 Divide the group in two. If possible in separate rooms.

GROUP A

  a Give group A forty Cuisenaire rods or a bunch of matches and some glue.
  b Tell them to build whatever they like with the rods or matches. Their structure must be self-supporting and only be made of rods or matches.
  c They have five minutes to complete the construction task.
  d After the structure has been built, they have ten minutes to write a brief report on how they proceeded in accomplishing their task.

7.11

LEVEL
Intermediate+

MATERIALS
A box of Cuisenaire rods or matches and glue, a common object like an umbrella or a Coca-Cola bottle, Report Evaluation sheets

TIME
45 minutes

FOCUS
Problem-solving, Discussing and writing

● Give the group the report evaluation sheet to guide them in writing up their reports (see page 131).
● Check that they understand vocabulary and procedure.
● The whole group works together to write up one report.
● Each member must then have a copy for the next stage of the activity.

GROUP B

a Give group B an object such as an umbrella or a Coca-Cola bottle.
b Tell them they have five minutes to brainstorm as many non-typical uses for this object as they can.
c After they have finished their brainstorming, they have ten minutes to write a brief report of how they proceeded in accomplishing their task.
● Give the group the report evaluation sheet to guide them in writing up their reports.
● Check that they understand vocabulary and procedure.
● The whole group works together to write up one report.
● Each member must then have a copy for the next phase of the activity.

2 Groups exchange tasks. Explain to each group what their new task is. Group A now does the brainstorming and group B the construction. Each group writes up reports on their new tasks.
3 Pair students from group A with students from group B.
4 Ask these pairs to compare their reports and to discuss the differences in each group's procedure for solving the problems. Encourage them to talk about their own feelings or opinions.
5 Bring the whole group back together and ask everyone to share something from their pairwork discussions.
6 Introduce the idea of 'open versus closed' thinking.
● Open thinking is what is involved in the construction task in that the builders are free to construct what they wish.
● Closed thinking means not being able to break out of pre-conceived ideas. Closed thinking is what must be avoided if the brainstormers are to find new uses for the umbrella or Coke bottle.
● Which is easier, open or closed thinking? Why?
7 Discuss how these ideas apply to their own work or company or to any firm in general. Why do the students think American companies would do this exercise with their managers?

ACKNOWLEDGEMENT
Ken Kasler, who is with the European School of Business Management in Paris, gave out this list in his exploitation of the Video Arts film 'Meetings, Bloody Meetings', produced and directed by John Cleese.

WORKSHEET FOR ACTIVITY 7.11

Report evaluation sheet

In writing up your reports, you should consider and include the following ideas when applicable:

1 How did your group decide what to build or think of new uses for the object?

2 What were the steps in the actual construction or brainstorming?

3 What were the roles each person played during the task?

4 In general, was the group as a whole: democratic but organised? autocratic? laissez-faire? just interested? really involved?

5 Below are roles sometimes assumed by members of a group working together. In your group who played which role?

Information-processor: this person receives information from the participants, analyses or interprets it, integrating it into the discussion.

Coordinator: this person regulates the discussion between participants, inviting opinions for or against, suggestions and additional facts.

Evaluator: this person expresses a personal judgement about the opinions and suggestions contributed by the other participants.

Harmoniser: this person tries to smooth over differences which may arise between participants and which can affect the climate of the group.

Gatekeeper: this person helps the coordinator to regulate the discussion by drawing in the silent and holding back the talkative.

Follower: this person goes along with the group's discussions and decisions. They contribute their agreement to group choices.

Blocker: this person disrupts the group's process by blocking progress on discussions or decisions. They do this by interrupting or putting up strong opposition or opinions.

Recognition-seeker: this person's aim is to be seen and heard at all costs.

Dominator: this person rules over the group much like a monarch. They try to regulate everything and to delegate nothing. Their will controls all progress.

Avoider: this person does not care about the group or the issue under debate. They are not part of the group.

7.12

LEVEL
Elementary+

MATERIALS
For each group of three to five students: a raw egg, two balloons, a ball of string, a roll of sellotape, two pieces of A4 paper and a floor cloth

TIME
20 minutes

FOCUS
Listening/ Speaking, Understanding and giving simple instructions

DON'T BREAK THE EGGS!

How to stand on a chair, hold your arm out straight and drop an egg without breaking it is the basis for this zany problem-solving activity.

Preparation

Bring the objects listed to class.

Procedure

1 Divide students up into small groups of three to five people.
2 Give each group the material described.
3 Tell students that they have ten minutes to find a way of dropping the egg from a pre-determined height (a student standing on a chair) without breaking it.
   In order to do this there are some rules. They are:
   ● Students can use all the material given them, but nothing else.
   ● Someone in each group must stand up on a chair, extend their arm out straight, and drop the egg onto the floor without breaking it.
   ● The egg must be dropped, not let down by the string. Otherwise any means can be used to protect the egg.
   ● Everyone speaks English while finding the solution.
   ● They must not try out their solution before their demonstration to the class (Step 4). Each group only gets one egg!
4 At the end of ten minutes, call time. Each group takes turns demonstrating their solution to the problem by dropping their egg.

NOTE
This is one of our favourites and we have seen it break the ice for even the most serious groups of students. It is the proof that business people really do like to have fun. The answer to its success lies in the fact that it is analogous to situations that actually occur in their professional lives.

Some groups enjoy explaining to each other how they found the solution to the problem. Some classes, especially ones of a more competitive spirit, like to have the best solution judged and a prize awarded.

ACKNOWLEDGEMENT
Our thanks to Judy Baker for sharing this activity with us and for all the fun and laughter it has brought into numerous classrooms.

CREATIVE THINKING

Here is a problem-solving activity for when you are stuck for ideas. It involves finding a solution to a problem by thinking of ways to achieve the opposite effect to the one you are looking for.

LEVEL
Upper
Intermediate

Procedure:

MATERIALS
None

1 As a warm-up to this activity, begin a discussion on creativity, its importance, and how to nurture it. (Or, if you feel it's more appropriate, you can have this discussion after the actual problem-solving activity.)

TIME
45 minutes

2 Explain to the group that they have come together to find a solution to a company problem. The problem is: Finding ways to spend more money. Ask them to explore ways of making things much more expensive. Encourage the group to get really wild. Give everyone a luxury company car! Enrol everyone in a health farm periodically!

FOCUS
Discussing and
creative problem-
solving

3 Once the idea takes hold and everyone is in full swing, switch over to exploring the opposite side of the issue. Tell the group their mission now is to come up with ways to cut costs.

4 As a follow-up ask students to take notes and prepare a report on the meeting to present in the next class.

RATIONALE

Flash the calendar back a decade. Imagine your life as it was then. There are big differences between then and now. How many can you find? Well, ten years ago there was probably no fax, no memory type-writer, no auto-dialer on the telephone. At home there was no micro-wave, no food processor, and probably not a VCR. Now come back to the present and breathe a deep sigh of relief. What moral can you draw from this? What about, 'if you characterise your future by what you are doing today, you will be in big trouble'? Nowadays it takes creative thinking to stay ahead. Creativity is no longer optional – it has become a survival skill. What is the difference between creative and non-creative people? Creative people have learned to pay attention to and nurture their ideas. They let their minds go with new ideas and try to take them farther. The good news is that everyone can learn to be more creative than they presently are. One technique to develop creativity is to break routine. This is an important one for us and for students. By breaking routines, we wake up dormant brain cells. 'Brainstorming' is a widely used technique to stimulate creativity. For brainstorming to be successful there must be rules. The central rule is no judging. Once the conscious mind starts criticising or judging it can bring creativity to a screeching halt. In using creativity in the classroom it is essential to separate the 'new idea' portion of the brain from the 'refining' part.

Here are four rules to follow in creative decision making/problem-solving:

- Put aside a specific slot of time.
- Just let ideas come.
- Do it without judgement.
- If possible don't do it alone, let your ideas bounce off those of others.

ONE-TO-ONE

Do this activity with you and your student stimulating each other's creative ideas.

Bibliography

Bandler, R, Grinder, J 1979 *Frogs into Princes* Real People Press

Bosworth-Gerome, S, Helye-Lebas, C and Marret, R 1987 *Lire l'Anglais Scientifique et Technique* Ellipses

Curran, C 1976 *Counseling Learning in Second Language* Apple River Press

Davis, P, and Rinvolucri, M 1990 *The Confidence Book* Longman

Dickinson, T, Leveque, A, Sagot, H 1976 *All's Well 2* Didier

Gattegno, C 1976 *The Common Sense of Teaching Foreign Languages* Educational Solutions

Gilbert, J B 1984 *Clear Speech* CUP

Jenkins, R 1989 *Tigers Don't Eat Grass* Ebury Press

Jones, L and Von Baeyer, C 1983 *Functions of American English* CUP

Lindstromberg, S 1990 *The Recipe Book* Longman

Maley, A and Duff, A 1982 *Drama Techniques in Language Learning* CUP

Morgan, J 'Empty Chair Roleplays' in Lindstromberg 1990, pp 42–43

Moskowitz, G 1978 *Caring and Sharing in the Foreign Language Classroom* Newbury House

Murphey, T 1990 *Teaching One to One* Longman

Mushashi, M 1974 *The Book of Five Rings* The Overlook Press

Postman, N and Weingarter, C 1977 *The Art of Subversive Teaching* Pitman

Rinvolucri, M 1985 *Grammar Games* CUP

Stevick, E 1980 *A Way and Ways* Rowley M.A. Newbury House

Stevick, E 1986 *Images and Options in the Language Classroom* CUP

Woodward, T 1990 *Models and Metaphors in Language Teacher Training* CUP; revised and expanded from *Loop Input* 1988 Pilgrims Publications